CRIMINAL REHABILITATION . . . WITHIN AND WITHOUT THE WALLS

CRIMINAL REHABILITATION . . .

WITHIN AND WITHOUT THE WALLS

WITH CONTRIBUTIONS FROM EXPERTS WITHIN THE FIELD

Edited by

EDWARD M. SCOTT, Ph.D.

Oregon Alcohol, Drug Treatment and Training Center
Clinic Director
Associate Clinical Professor of Psychiatry
University of Oregon Medical School
Portland, Oregon

and

KATHRYN L. SCOTT, B.S.

With a Foreword by
GEORGE A. VanHOOMISSEN
Dean
The National College of District Attorneys
College of Law
University of Houston
Houston, Texas

CHARLES C THOMAS • PUBLISHER

Springfield, Illinois U.S.A.

Published and Distributed Throughout the World by

CHARLES C THOMAS • PUBLISHER

BANNERSTONE HOUSE

301-327 East Lawrence Avenue, Springfield, Illinois, U.S.A.

© 1973, by CHARLES C THOMAS • PUBLISHER
ISBN O-398-02730-7
Library of Congress Catalog Card Number: 72-92178

Printed in the United States of America
PP-22

DEDICATION

To our children Kathleen, Mike, Maureen, Tim and Molly whom we hope will never become criminals; but if they do, they could be rehabiliated.

CONTRIBUTORS

Bird, Gordon, M.A. Senior Counselor, D.V.R., Portland (Oregon) Work Release Centers

Colback, Edward, M.D. Director, Family Crisis Project, Portland, Oregon

Copeland, Sharon J., M.S.W. Chief Social Worker, Drug Treatment and Training Project, Alcohol and Drug Section, Portland, Oregon

Fosterling, Charles, M.S.W. Coordinator, Family Crisis Project, Portland, Oregon

Hoffstetter, William, M.A. Director of Treatment Services, Drug Treatment and Training Project, Alcohol and Drug Section, Portland, Oregon

Mitchell, John Attorney General of the United States

Owens, Roger D., M.A., (Ph.D candidate) Coordinator of Diagnostic Services, Oregon Problem Drinker Traffic Fatality Project, Alcohol and Drug Section

Reed, Amos E. Administrator, Corrections Division, State of Oregon

Roth, Phillip P. Judge, Circuit Court, Fourth Judicial District, Multnomah County, Portland, Oregon

Scott, Edward M., Ph.D. Director, Oregon Alcohol and Drug Treatment and Training Center, Portland, Oregon

Scott, Kathryn L., B.S. Active in Community Organizations

Tyler, Stanley T. Rehabilitation Counselor, Department of Psychiatry, Veteran's Administration Hospital, Salt Lake City, Utah

Warren, Lieutenant Myron Chief of Detectives, Multnomah County Sheriff's Office, Portland, Oregon

FOREWORD

About twenty years ago I became acquainted with a young psychologist named Ed Scott. Over the years, first in my capacity as a defense attorney, then as a legislator and finally as a prosecutor, I have admired Dr. Scott's broad perspective and interest in every aspect of criminal justice.

CRIMINAL REHABILITATION is an excellent example of that perspective and the editors' understanding of the fundamental principle that no single individual, agency or discipline can ever accomplish system-wide reform or rehabilitation.

Rehabilitation of offenders will only be accomplished when all of the components of the criminal justice system begin to communicate and cooperate with each other. Even then, police, prosecutors, defense, courts and correctional personnel cannot effect significant improvement without the understanding and support of others. Certainly other agencies and individuals in society have a role and responsibility as well.

This book is on the right track. It's approach is sound. The contributors are all practitioners, and many are specialists with long experience in the field. Each brings his own experience and insight into the larger problem area. The result is a practical and valuable collection of information, experience, statistics and theories which should appeal to the specialist and generalist.

With increasing emphasis at long last being placed upon the importance of corrections, it is important that practical works such as CRIMINAL REHABILITATION be made available not only to those professionals who specialize in corrections, but to others who labor in the fields of criminal justice. The general public, whose interest in corrections has been awakened in recent months, can find much in this book to stimulate its interest and to awaken its mind to significant obstacles to rehabilitation and opportunities for improvement of the system.

CRIMINAL REHABILITATION is both timely and informative. It is unique in its scope and approach. It should be fascinating reading for a large audience of concerned citizens.

George A. Van Hoomissen
Dean, National College of District Attorneys
College of Law
University of Houston
Houston, Texas 77004

PREFACE

This collection of articles is an attempt to present a practical and *rounded view* of the difficulties and some of the solutions for the rehabilitation of criminals.

Specifically, we have tried to avoid the following:

1. A global, simplistic explanation and solution for either the causes of crime or the solution regarding rehabilitation of criminals.

2. *Theory-building* without a foundation in application.

3. The *missing link* approach; namely, if only *this one thing* is done all will be solved.

4. That one professional group—psychologists, psychiatrists, social workers, rehabilitation counselors, clergy, ex-convicts, political figures, or the law—has *the* answer.

5. Bitterness and defeatism of others who have tried, but failed in the fight against crime.

Hence, we have included a wide circle of individuals, all endeavoring to *make-a-point.* Hopefully, from this panoramic view, with an appropriate amount of vision, theory, and practical application, an accurate and effective approach to one of our country's biggest problems—the rehabilitation of criminals will emerge.

Perhaps the following vignette illustrates the spirit of this volume. Cousins (1971) reported, "Shortly after his (Pope John XXIII) election he set out from the Vatican one morning on the first of visits to Italian prisons. Asked by his aides his purpose, he said simply: 'It is somewhat more difficult for prisoners to come to see me.'"*

*Cousins, N.: The improbable triumvirate. *Sat. Review.,* Oct., 1971, p. 24-35.

ACKNOWLEDGMENTS

At this time an expression of appreciation is given to Charles C Thomas, Publisher. Mr. Payne Thomas's entire staff has been most helpful, kind and professional in this, as in other works they have published for me. The editors of this volume express a most sincere *thank you*. A special note of appreciation is given to Mr. Payne Thomas, who has always been most encouraging, considerate and helpful.

E.M.S.
K.L.S.

CRIMINAL REHABILITATION . . .
WITHIN AND WITHOUT THE WALLS

SECTION ONE
ORIENTATION

CHAPTER I

AN OVERVIEW OF CRIME: A SMORGASBORD OF CAUSES AND SOLUTIONS

EDWARD M. AND KATHRYN L. SCOTT

PERHAPS THE MAIN trouble with a cliche is the tendency to offer half-truths. For instance, *The squeaky wheel gets the oil* is true only if someone hears or if someone cares.

It seems that, one of the *squeaky wheels* of our society—prisons —is being heard, suddenly, by everyone. A natural consequence emerges in which almost everyone, including numerous organizations, insist, that their *oil* is the correct solution to the enormous, complex problem of crime prevention and rehabilitation.

In this rather brief overview, our purpose is to present a few of the diagnoses and solutions emerging from a variety of sources all aimed at either preventing crime, correcting the prison system or rehabilitation programs.

Mrs. Barbara Greene has gained national recognition for her efforts at changing the interior design of prisons. In an interview given to Charlotte Graydon, Mrs. Greene (1971) stated, "I do not believe that the prison experience should be a punishing one, but a rehabilitation one."

Goldfarb and Singer (1971) concentrate on the prison system itself saying, "The American prison system as a two hundred-year-old experiment in correction, has failed."

Hollie (1971) presents the views of several judges across the U.S.A. who actively oppose sentencing individuals. As an illustration, Hollie quotes from Judge Augustine of New Orleans District

5

Court, "The system is medieval and archaic. I can't under my oath of office tolerate the situation as it is."

While, sociologist Schur (1969) in his book, entitled, *Our Criminal Society,* offers the thesis that the economic ills. ". . . lie at the very heart of the most serious crime in the United States today."

Skinner (1971) voices an even clearer and more sweeping generality when he writes, "A scientific analysis shifts the credit as well as the blame to the environment . . ." In his view, individuals respond according to their environment, and efforts should be made to change the environment, not the individual. The individual will respond to the changes made in the environment.

A different emphasis is given by Anderson (1971) who reports on police corruption. Anderson highlighted that mayors of large cities must rely on the police, ". . . to keep the city running well. . . ." The mayor is therefore reluctant to face the issue of police corruption.

Perhaps Slater (1970) put the matter squarely when he noted that numerous people who settled in this country were not successful in confronting problems in their own country. Such individuals, according to Slater, tend to be selfish and place money ". . . ahead of love and loyalty; but most important, when faced with a difficult situation . . . tended to chuck the whole thing . . ."

Professor Clendenen (1971) feels that upgrading the inmate's self-concept within the prison, would greatly improve correctional programs.

Other individuals suggest total change. One such individual is Waskow (1972) who states, "Forget about reform; it's time to talk about abolishing jails and prisons in American society." Waskow is a resident fellow at the Institute for Police Studies and offers two alternatives for the prison system:

1. A *fenced-off town* or farm in which life is normal in all respects. In this *town* are violent criminals. It is open to all, *invited* by the residents.
2. A kibbutz-like community.

Robins (1966) did a follow-up of individuals, who as children had been in trouble with the law and later as adults were sent to prison. In her summary of effective factors associated with *success;* it was found, "A sizeable proportion of these subjects did improve late in their adult careers sometimes attributed that improvement to a fear of further punishment or to loyalty to their spouses."

Certain areas are receiving more attention; these are commonly termed *victimless crimes* or crimes without victims. Regardless of the names, this category includes laws against sex, gambling, and drugs. It is argued that in these areas, the so-called *victim* is willing—he bets, buys drugs, or solicits a prostitute. Although as Newsweek (1971) pointed out, pimps and prostitutes have become growingly aggressive. Among the issues is that of time and money spent in these areas, while rape, robbery and murder *flourish.*

Smith and Pollack (1971) argue that the price we pay, ". . . in corruption, the denial of civil liberties, and overburdening of our criminal justice system . . . isn't worth it—besides certain kinds of behavior can't be controlled by law."

No one professional group has all the answers. Dershowitz (1969) notes that

> Over this past year, with the help of two researchers, I conducted a thorough survey of all the published literature on prediction of antisocial conduct. We read and summarized many hundred articles, monographs, and books. Surprisingly enough, we were able to discover fewer than a dozen studies which followed up psychiatric predictions of antisocial conduct. And even more surprisingly, these few studies strongly suggest that psychiatrists were rather inaccurate predictors—inaccurate in an absolute sense, and even less accurate when compared with other professionals, such as psychologists, social workers, and correctional officials; and when compared to actuarial devices, such as prediction or experience tables. Even more significant for legal purposes, it seems that psychiatrists are particularly prone to one type of error—overprediction. They tend to predict antisocial conduct in many instances where it would not, in fact, occur. Indeed, our research suggests that for every correct psychiatric prediction of violence, there are numerous erroneous predictions. That is, among every group of inmates presently confined on the basis of psychiatric predictions of violence, there are only a few who would, and many more who would not, actually engage in such conduct if released.

The importance of this finding by Dershowitz stresses that no one group of professionals has the answer. What is needed is the cooperation of the most skilled individuals in all professional groups, joining hands, in cooperation with all other therapeutic potentials—volunteers, aides, clergy, ex-cons, etc.

Some rather major changes appear to be forthcoming. One such change is happening with the United States Parole Board. In the past, this Board did not have to give its reason to the prisoner, nor his lawyer if he had one, for making a negative decision. Now, the United States Parole Board will give reasons to the inmates denied parole.

Parole is one of the main avenues to freedom for prisoners as can be seen from the following figures:

1. In 1970, nearly 40% of the men released from federal prisons were out through the parole channel.
2. In 1970, more than 60% of the men on a state level, were released from prison by the parole route.

Gumpert (1972) who interviewed Mr. Reed, Chairman of the U.S. Parole Board, quoted Reed as saying ". . . there will be a check-off list of fourteen possible reasons, with room for a Parole Board member to write in other reasons. Prison caseworkers will show prisoners the list and add interpretations, based on what they know to be in a prisoner's life."

The student wanting a total view of the entire problem of crime—its theory, evaluation of programs, suggestion for improvement, etc., will find a recent three volume work edited by Radzinowicz and Wolfgang, entitled Crime and Justice (1971) a valuable source of information.

Finally, the report by the President's Commission on Law Enforcement and Administration of Justic entitled, *The Challenge of Crime in a Free Society*, is a work that should be secured by interested readers.

REFERENCES

1. Anderson, D.: Police crime: more than rotten apples. *Wall Street Journal*, Nov. 22, p. 12, 1971.
2. Clendenen, R.: What's the matter with corrections? *Federal Probation*, 25:8-12, 1971.

3. Dershowitz, A.: The psychiatrist's power in civil commitment. *Psychology Today*, Feb. 1969. Copywright C. Communications/Research/ Machines, Inc.

4. Goldfarb, R. and Singer, Linda: Disaster road: the American prison system. *Intellrctual Digest*, 4:19-23, 1971.

5. Greene, Barbara: Remarks from an interview with Charlotte Graydon, appearing in the *Oregonian*, Nov. 20, Section 2M, 1971.

6. Gumpert, D.: Masters of fate. *Wall Street Journal*, Jan. 14, p. 1, 1972.

7. Hollie, Pamela: Legal action: judges across the U.S. campaign for reforms in the nation's prisons. *Wall Street Journal*, Nov. 3, p. 1, 1971.

8. *Newsweek*, Nov. 29, p. 83, 1971.

9. Radzinowicz, L. and Wolfgang, M.: *Crime and Justice*. Basic Books, New York, 1971.

10. Robins, Lee: *Deviant Children Grown Up*. Williams and Wilkins Co., Baltimore, 1966.

11. Schur, E.: *Our Criminal Society*. Prentice-Hall, Englewood Cliffs, 1969.

12. Skinner, B.: *Beyond Freedom and Dignity*. Alfred A. Knopf, New York, 1971.

13. Slater, P.: *The Pursuit of Loneliness*. Beacon Press, Boston, 1970.

14. Smith, A. and Pollack, Harriet: Crimes without victims. *Saturday Review*, Dec. 4, pp. 27-29, 1971.

15. Waskow, A.: I am not free. *Saturday Review*, Jan. 8, pp. 20-21, 1972.

CHAPTER II

ADMINISTRATION OF CORRECTIONAL PROGRAMS

Amos E. Reed

M UCH HAS BEEN written about the administration of correctional departments, divisions, sections and their unit parts. The information given and conclusions drawn tend toward gross oversimplification of an extremely complex subject. Seen through the eyes of an executive head of corrections, the subject is anything but simple.

Instant and total expertise is professed by some legislators, political executives, judges, members of the news media, clients, ex-clients, and the public. While annoying, and occasionally helpful, the efforts of these naive, inexperienced and grossly uninformed citizens are, at least, understandable. What is most harmful is the result of the pontificating of social and behavioral scientists who speak with such precise exactness and challenge, that they mislead thousands, as well as themselves.

Secondly, executives are held responsible for programs, staff performance and client cure when, in fact, they have limited resources and tools for accomplishing the exacting assignments given to them, as suggested by the Joint Commission on Correctional Manpower (1969). Frameworks of law, tradition, rules, regulations, multiple and conflicting expectations, and inadequate budgets function to frustrate the most highly trained and experienced administrators.

The public image of an administrator, warden or superintendent of a corrections agency is that of one who possesses total, almost god-like powers, authority, and resources.] He is seen as one who has, or can get, answers and results with the precision of a chemist or engineer.] There is little or no awareness of just how inexact the correctional program is or of how executives are buffeted and limited by a multitude of conflicting interests and expectations.

Almost any assumption made or conclusion drawn concerning corrections administration is subject to challenge. Some, but not all, are highly motivated to help the clients entrusted to their care. Some, but not the majority, are adequately knowledgeable about causation, etiology, and treatment of offenders and their problems. Few have the managerial *moxey* to motivate, originate, develop, and administer the interlocking component parts of the complex systems assigned to their professional and managerial responsibility.

[Since many administrators seem to be chosen in relation to politics, personality, professed but grossly lacking knowledge, seniority, charisma, or promises of unattainable results, it is a near miracle that corrections agencies can function at all.] Unprovable claims of messianic power and insight lead decision-makers down primrose paths to the thorny patches of reality. But this seems not to deter the decision-makers from backing away, making repeated errors in selection and proceeding to follow the next pseudo-professional piper who next happens along. This bumbling process is seen at every level. Attempts are made to avoid this bumbling process by placing the thorny crown of total responsibility upon the executive when, in fact, a horde of persons should bear a fair share of responsibility for irrational, irresponsible and erratic support of unproven *causes*.

I am reminded of Isaac Watts (1807), who observed, "So weak and unhappy is human nature that it is ever ready to run into extremes and when we would recover ourselves from an excess on the right hand, we know not where to stop till we are got to an excess on the left."

[Administrators should be chosen because of their demonstrated professional and leadership abilities. Integrity, maturity, courage, experience and general ability, should not be subordinated to some array of academic degrees that *may* only prove that a man is something that he isn't. Education is fine, even necessary, but it is no substitute for character, ability and experience.]

Provision should be made for clearly delineating expectations, for providing human and material resources for a service delivery system, and for developing a client information system that can give the executives the timely feedback of information necessary of relating results to efforts[7]. The debt of failures in these areas rests heavily upon the general citizenry, but most heavily upon the clients whose needs are inadequately and inappropriately met. Excessive prices can be paid for foolish extremes, of innovation unsupported by frameworks of tested policy and procedure. These are not just prices in relation to money, but also *prices* in the lives of criminals.

[The good administrator will consider his multiple assignments, assess expectations against resources, and then proceed to draw upon all interested sources for assistance in developing dynamic management and treatment designs for realistically accomplishing]the array of assignments presented to him, as indicated in the Final Report of Joint Commission on Correctional Manpower and Training, published under the title, *A TIME TO ACT*, Wash. D.C., 1969.

Inventories of resources should go far beyond the parent agency and its component parts. High perspective and vision will train one to think in wholistic, eclectic terms involving peer agencies, supportive volunteer and general citizen action, clients and their significant supporters, labor, industry, business, news media, all branches of government—everyone and everything that may be challenged and involved as resources. Doing all this, while keeping the ship on an even keel, is no assignment for a novice.

Just as the client's self-image is important, so too is the agency's image to itself and to others. Overclaims of knowledge and success may fool others for a time. But the day of reckoning always follows[5]. There is no substitute for good stewardship, professionally and managerially. Sustained support will tend to flow to the courageous administrator who shares information good and bad, *speaks honestly*, leads aggressively and dynamically, and challenges the involvement of all in the serious tasks assigned to him.

It is essential that program managers see each person—client, staff, general citizen—as one who is unique, one who has dignity as a human being, and is worthy of our best efforts to sustain, assist, encourage, and, where necessary, direct. To achieve this awareness, it is necessary to study the person gainst the backdrop of his life, experiences and culture. In so doing, it soon becomes apparent that *treatment* must be individualized and selective.

[Our goal should be to assist the offending client to move away from residential dependency, through partial dependency to self support that is minimally acceptable to the general community]

Ideally, each child would receive the very best chance to develop his talents and potentials as a person. He would receive, firm but loving care from relatives, friends and associates to the degree that the care would have significance in the development of his (personality and character] The participants in his life development would become significant persons affecting the (development of a meaningful self-image along with an acceptable identification with the group—society as a whole] Security would counterbalance insecurity;] love would counterbalance rejection;] there would be acceptable life movement from the childhood to maturity. Agency personnel would learn to detect *gaps* in personality and character and would move to marshall all available resources to implement remedial action, as pointed out in the United States President's Commission on Law Enformement and Administration of Justice, published in *THE CHALLENGE OF CRIME IN A FREE SOCIETY* (1967).

Early detection of problems accompanied with early corrective action would insure the most effective redirection of life styles. Public and private agencies would be supported in their attempts at prompt, healing action. Sadly for all concerned, problems must multiply and move to extreme in order to attract attention resulting in delayed action. [By this time, the person has, too frequently, developed set patterns of antisocial behavior, distrust of helpers and a self-image of failure—the *born to lose* syndrome.]

(The corrections administrator must assess the needs of his clients against the needs and resources of the general community and give leadership in efforts to bring about behavior changes satisfactory to the clients, as well as their responsive reaction to law and custom.]

[Every effort must be expended to move the offender toward

acceptable self-support.] Community resources have to be developed in a spirit of cooperation with local agencies. In fact, local agencies must be assisted to develop their own array of therapies and agencies.

The state agency must play a leadership role without stifling or supplanting local initiative. Consultation, advice, standard-setting, inspection for compliance with law, training, etc., are roles available to the state. When government and professional groups can reasonably agree, moves may be made to regional or state program management. Such systems and changes should not introduce bureaucracy and pressures that create and multiply further delays in meeting needs. Reasonable and experienced participants will share in the decisions to allocate resources and assign responsibility.

Having determined needs, inventoried and allocated resources, and assigned responsibilities, multiple goals will be identified. Evaluation and research may weed out the less desirable, emphasize the productive and lend support to attempts to retain and expand resources.

The Correctional Administrator's Source Book (1967) suggests that statutes should be revised and modified to provide maximum administrative flexibility while insuring good stewardship and accountability. Partnership should be established with the representatives of the various branches of government and the analyst specialists who must monitor programs and advise the decision-makers.

There is a need for agencies to develop and publish clearly understandable statements of philosophy[1]. Basic policy and procedure should be developed, published and revised in response to changing needs. These efforts should be aimed at opening opportunities for reformation and self-expression rather than attempting to be vindictive, punitive and repressive[3].

Clear channels of responsibility should be established. It is a myth that there is freedom without framework. The syrupy permissiveness of the immature, false professionals can do irreparable harm to individuals and to groups. Likewise, the overly rigid, unyielding, coldly punitive person can be just as damaging. Therefore, [managers and personnel officers should select persons of integrity, maturity, experience, flexibility and *heart.* These latter persons can respond to learning experience, are not so threatened by change and are seen by all as persons of substance to be trusted with the important tasks assigned to them.

Administrators will proceed to align their resources, map their procedures and goals, build in evaluation, respond to needed change, and communicate carefully to all who will listen. They, in turn, will be responsive to leadership, experience and instruction.

Within the atmosphere of philosophy and framework set forth in the preceding paragraphs, the administrator will face the daily tasks with an optimistic and courageous attitude, knowing that his efforts will merit the support of clients and co-workers. The specialists and subordinate managers will keep their houses in order and all will work for the common good. Corrective action can be taken in a nonthreatening manner. Initiative and creativity will flourish in this rich soil of human concern.

Any attempt to exercise professional decision-making, to observe constitutional rights and to be effectively responsive to citizen needs runs head on into an unbelievable array of currents and riptides of decision-making by multiple jurisdictions. Police, district attorneys, defense attorneys, grand juries, multiple courts, governmental administrative officers and staff, parole and probation departments, corrections actions, ad infinitum. All jurisdictions and interests must be recognized and observed, public and personal interests considered, and actions taken in considerate and timely ways, or severe legal and professional prices are paid.

The executive decision-maker must attempt to be responsive to the known needs of all parties while constantly remaining on the alert of the need for system change, the need to detect and eliminate faults and the need to expedite client movement through the system.

Administrators, managers, and professionals of all degrees have the burden of shared responsibility to communicate information helpful to the general public in avoiding and preventing antisocial behavior and social ills of all nature. Substantial reduction of social ills must start *early* (in childhood) and be sustained through the developmental years of personality and character formation. Special attention must be paid to the stormy years of adolescence and to those children and youth who present unusual behavior or needs. Crisis points may arise at any time in a person's life. How we respond to these needs is critical to the individuals involved and to the groups of which they are a part. Corrections administrators, their peers and associates must share their knowledge and experience with parents, teachers, ministers and the general public. To fail in this is to function ineffectively and to perform inadequately.

There are many sources of detailed information concerning management of correctional institutions and agencies. The reader is referred to the Federal Bureau of Prisons which has developed many fine manuals of operations such as the one on *Institutional Sanitation* by Graham Walton, Ph.D., Sanitary Engineer, U.S. Public Health Service.

Inquiries addressed to the National Council on Crime and Delinquency, the American Corrections Associations, or to state departments and divisions will usually bring information and materials concerning specific subject matter. The Library of Congress, state and local libraries are most generous and helpful to the executive or general citizen in search of information and help. State and private universities, United Fund offices and similar sources can be most helpful.

It is the duty of corrections administrators to become acquainted with professional and management information and trends. The development and dissemination of information is a very important subject. Libraries must develop to provide audio-visual aids and every other possible means helpful to (inform the (public of) agency philosophy, law, and (program progress.)

It is abundantly clear that the present-day corrections administrator is no longer involved in a simple corrections system that calls for holding men in confinement for a period of time and then releasing them to their home communities without accounting for time, programs and dollars. The old *hardline* approach is rapidly becoming a thing of the past[8]. In its place is the rapidly developing interlocking system of programs and accountability that staggers the mind to comprehend.

(No longer can the administrator serve as a god-like person of total power and wisdom whose word is law and whose actions are unquestioned] [Today, he must be educated, experienced, a well-trained generalist capable of utilizing appropriate strategies and synchronizing the efforts of a host of line and staff assistants as they, in turn, work in concert with all other interested persons, *including the clients.*]

Although held fully responsible for the actions of all staff and clients, the corrections administrator very early gains an awareness of his dependence upon others. [Management becomes a shared responsibility with a division of labor.]

On any given day in 1972, the State of Oregon houses two thousand felons and provides probation and parole services to an additional five thousand men and women. Furthermore, presentence and other services are provided to courts, parole boards, and other agencies of government.

Interlocking compacts provide for reciprocal service, information and resources among most of the fifty states and the United States Bureau of Prisons. Special contracts between the United States Bureau, California, Idaho and Washington make institutions and support services mutually available. This cooperation is most helpful to the clients and to all branches of the criminal justice system.

Oregon law makes it possible to provide forestry camps, community centers and other state services available to counties and cities on a contractual basis. This is in recognition of the need for taxpayers to get the greatest possible return for their dollar investment in rehabilitation resources and provides an expanded range of alternative programs for offenders. It should be noted that use of regional resources, reciprocal service by contract, and the general pooling of effort are most healthy signs on the corrections scene. States are playing increasingly heavy leadership roles in updating, coordinating, standardizing and directing corrections systems at all levels of government within the states.

REFERENCES

1. *American Journal of Corrections*, American Correctional Association, Washington, D.C., Volume 34, No. 1, January, February 1972.
2. *A Time to Act*, Final Report of Joint Commission on Correctional Manpower and Training, Washington, D.C., 1969.

3. *Constitution of Oregon,* Article I, Section 15. Adopted February 14, 1959.
4. *Correctional Administrator's Source Book,* American Correctional Association, Washington, D.C., 1967, Vol. II.
5. *Manual of Correctional Standards,* American Correctional Association, Washington, D.C., 1966.
6. Nelson, E. K.: *Developing Correctional Administrators,* Report of the Joint Commission on Correctional Manpower and Training, Washington, D.C., 1969.
7. *Priorities for Law Enforcement,* 1970. Comprehensive Plan, Oregon Law Enforcement Council, Salem, Oregon, May 1970.
8. *State-Local Relations in the Criminal Justice System,* Advisory Committee on Intergovernmental Relations, Washington, D.C., Aug. 1971.
9. *The Challenge of Crime in a Free Society,* U.S. President's Commission on Law Enforcement and Administration of Justice, 1967.
10. Watts, I.: *The Mind,* Benington, 1809.

SECTION TWO
LEGAL ASPECTS

CHAPTER III

SENTENCING:
A VIEW FROM THE BENCH

PHILLIP J. ROTH

GUILTY

THE ATTORNEY FINISHES the plea for clemency which his role as advocate demands.

The offender stands up.

The offender may or may not state his own plea for clemency.

The judge looks at the offender straight in the eye. The judge is ready to impose sentence. That sentence may be from

". . . therefore, I hereby sentence you to . . ." one day to life in jail. The judge may suspend the imposition of sentence and place the offender on probation. The probation may have conditions: anything from serving a year in jail, to going back to school, to staying out of an area of the state, to refraining from practicing a business or profession.

When the offender stands up to hear the sentence, the judge already knows what that sentence is going to be. Depending upon the charge and the offender involved, the judge may have spent from a couple of hours to many days pondering what sentence to mete out. It is not uncommon for a judge to lay awake nights thinking about a person who must be sentenced. Sometimes a judge only has to worry about what is best for the individual, but more often, the judge also has to worry about what is best for society. If it is difficult to decide what is best for the individual under a given set of circumstances, it is much more

21

difficult to balance the best interests of the individual *and* those of society.

". . . therefore, I hereby sentence you to . . ."

The next few words of a judge are of great importance to the offender. What makes a judge say those next few words? What goes through the judge's mind before reaching the conclusion as to what words to use next?

In understanding why the judge uses some words (life, sixty days, probation, suspended sentence), and not others, we must consider certain factors: the offender, the crime that was committed, the statutory requirements that affect the specific crime and the specific person involved, society, and the judge who is about to pronounce the sentence.

Many authorities in the area of penology tend to forget the importance of the role played by the judge. The judge, however, is very important in any consideration of our penal system, because

". . . therefore, I hereby sentence you to . . ." the trial judge stands at the threshold of the convicted person's entrance into the penal system as the enforcer of sanctions under the laws. Though in appearance the judge is merely a conduit in the execution of sanctions, in reality he possesses, in the absence of mandatory penalties, a god-like discretion in a spectrum ranging from the mild bench probation to the stiff imposition of the maximum penalty of incarceration under the applicable law for the specific crime involved.

When the judge has discretionary powers, which is the case in most instances, that judge should appreciate and understand the alternatives available to the judge in seeking to square justice with both society and the offender.

But how does, or how can, a judge appreciate and understand the alternatives available? Judges generally understand the basic needs and desires of society, unless they erroneously believe that as judges they are, or ought to be, better than the society in which they live. Judges who do not understand their role and function in our society should not be judges. It is beyond the scope of this chapter, however, to discuss those judges. Understanding the alternatives available from the standpoint of the offender is much more difficult for the judge.

A judge ought to know, but seldom does, what the offender will face after

". . . therefore, I hereby sentence you to . . ." the sentence is announced. A judge normally does not know what the offender will face after sentencing because the judiciary has too long adhered to the *Hands Off Policy* which is based on the court's aloofness from any practical concern with prisoners. That policy has been described by Eugene Barken (Counsel to the Federal Bureau of Prisons) as follows: "A court which imposes terms of imprisonment not knowing what kind of treatment and facilities await the defendant, is the same as a physician who prescribes not knowing the makeup or consequence of the drug." Or stated in the con's language: "Man, it is like if the courts were dispensing tickets for a round trip to purgatory, never having seen the place or consulted with the management."

A judge who does not know what prisons have to offer to the offender cannot make an adequate evaluation of the alternatives that are available to the offender. To understand these alternatives, we ought to strive for more involvement by judges with prison authorities. Perhaps it would be a good idea to require judges, as is done in some countries, to visit in jail the persons they have committed. Those visits may give the judges a better perspective of what may be the possible effect of the sentences that they mete out.

The State Trial Judges College in Nevada provides judges attending their course an opportunity to clinically discuss the real nature of the correctional system. That program consists of seminars in which judges, convicts, penologists and correctional authorities have a free *give and take* with each other. For a judge, those sessions are a rare opportunity to actually evaluate the force and quality of his jurisdiction when he sends a person to the penitentiary. In order to have a well-rounded judge, intellectually and emotionally, not physically, we ought to require that he participate in those programs more often. If we demand that teachers, correctional authorities, doctors and others continue their education in order to keep their positions, then perhaps we ought to demand the same of judges.

If we do not, how then can a judge rationally evaluate a punishment without sensing, as a human being himself, what that prison, and that term will accomplish, for good or for evil, for that offender and for society? Of course judges must send men to prison, but the option should be broader than mere caging. Judges must know the consequences of their sentences. They must also help to evolve and utilize the greater range of options that should exist.

Assuming that the judge is aware, because of his studies, participation and concern of what the offender will face, the next step is to consider the possibilities available under the law. In some instances the law requires a mandatory sentence, so the judge has little discretion to exercise. The legislature, and not the judge, decides on the sentence. More commonly, however, the legislature provides that the judge may impose the sentence that the judge finds to be fit for the particular individual.

When the judge has wide discretionary powers, then the next step is to look at the specific crime involved. It would be very difficult to classify each crime within a definite category, but judges sometimes find it helpful to divide crimes into three loosely defined categories: (1) crimes that threaten society; (2) crimes that are directed at an individual; and (3) crimes without victims.

As stated above, these categories are loosely defined. I shall mention a specific crime for each category, even when it might be argued ad infinitum whether or not each crime falls within the correct category, or even if they are the best of examples.

As illustrated of the first category (crimes which threaten society) we can utilize armed robbery. For the second category (crimes against an individual), we have crimes of passion. Finally, crimes without victims include such crimes as certain sexual relationships among consenting adults.

It is obvious that society has its smallest concern or interest in crimes without victims. It is in the other two categories, especially the first, that a judge needs to take into account society's interests.

Before going further, I should mention what society's interests presently are. They are rehabilitation, deterrence, and punishment. Ideally our society with its present state of technology, should be able to use criminal sentencing for rehabilitation only and use other methods for deterrence. Criminal sentences for the purpose of punishment should have disappeared with the covered wagon. In reality, our society has not been able to apply its advanced technology to penology, and as a consequence punishment is the effect of most sentences. Very few people believe in the deterrence effect of sentences. Rehabilitation in our present prison system today is in many instances achieved not because of the system, but in spite of it. So when a judge is going to ". . . therefore, I hereby sentence you to . . ." sentence a person, the first step must be to consider if the offender is rehabilitable. The judge usually makes this important decision by studying the nature of the crime, by itself, and in conjunction with the information available about the offender. In crimes such as sexual crimes involving consenting adults, generally there is no available means of rehabilitation. If the crime, on the other hand, still a crime without victims, involved alcoholism, then the judge may have available some sources for rehabilitating the offender. In the case of a crime involving alcoholism there is no longer need to use the sentencing process for deterrence or punishment. Society is finally beginning to recognize alcoholism as a sickness and not as a crime. Sentencing an offender in this category to jail accomplishes nothing for the offender or for society. Only when everything else fails will the judge send an offender in this category to jail. The exception is the offender who needs to *dry out* under supervision. The judge usually will suspend the imposition of sentence and place the offender on probation. In this type of case, the judge will normally impose some conditions on the offender as a prerequisite for probation. Those conditions, if properly selected, and with the cooperation of the offender, may result in the offender's rehabilitation. But the judge must consider carefully the sources available, the conditions to be imposed on the offender, and the attitude of the offender. If the judge properly balances those three elements, there is hope that the offender will be rehabilitated.

The most important of these three elements is not as some people believe, the attitude of the offender, but the sources available to the judge. In the last analysis, even if the offender has a poor attitude, but the judge has good sources available and he properly selects the conditions of probation, the chances of success are greater than if the offender has a good attitude but the judge has poor sources available for rehabilitation and the conditions of probation are not what the specific offender needs. More on this subject will be discussed later.

Moving next to the classification of crimes against an individual, we find that a judge in this type of case has more limited avenues. Crimes in this classification are generally a once-in-a-lifetime affair. Unless a judge faces a repeater, the judge will consider the offender's case more as a blow which fate has dealt to that individual rather than as a crime. An example of such an instance is the case when a person kills a spouse. In this type of crime, very often the offender has had no previous criminal record. This type of crime occurs more as an act of desperation than as an intended crime. Thus, when

". . . therefore, I hereby sentence you to . . ." sentencing the offender, the judge is faced with the following problem: the individual involved does not need to be rehabilitated. A crime such as killing one's spouse normally involves a momentarily demented mind. Nothing that the judge may do will have any effect in deterring others in similar circumstances. So what is left? Punishment!

But is punishment the proper disposition? It should be pointed out that the greatest punishment to someone who has killed a spouse is the sudden realization of the act. Nothing that society may do, directly or through a judge, is going to increase that punishment. Outside punishment can never be compared with the self-inflicted internal punishment of the offender.

The judge is placed in an impossible position

". . . therefore, I hereby sentence you . . ." because he cannot use the sentencing process either to rehabilitate, to deter crime, or to punish (even if the judge was induced, for whatever reason, to punish the offender).

Fortunately for some judges, but not the case for those who feel differently, in instances such as the one where a person is convicted of first degree murder for killing a spouse, the legislature has imposed the mandatory sentence of life. The judge's decisions

". . . therefore, I hereby sentence you to . . ." may, and are, very painful and frustrating for a judge.

Judges frequently ask themselves what can be accomplished by sending a particular offender to a penal institution. Assuming the judge has the power of using an alternative to jail, what are those alternatives? In some cases there is no alternative, and in other cases the alternatives, again depending on the crime, may be limited to such programs as the work release program. But is this enough? Is this all we owe to the offender, to ourselves, and mainly to society? I don't think so.

Before a course of action is proposed, we must deal with the last category or classification that I referred to above. That classification involves crimes which threaten society. Without going into the issue of whether one specific crime correctly falls within this category, let us assume for the purpose of this analysis that some acts, crimes, fall within this category.

When the judge faces the offender and looks straight in the offender's eye,

". . . therefore, I hereby sentence you to . . ." the judge should have only one thought in mind: rehabilitation.

Punishment should enter the judge's mind only when expert advice recommends that one of the tools involved in rehabilitating the specific individual is punishment. Punishment, for the sake of punishment, does not serve either the individual involved, or society. Punishment is useful only, if at all, as part of rehabilitation. The deterrence effects on an individual's sentence, if any, are so limited that deterrence seldom enters the judge's mind. Deterrence as a tool only enters a judge's mind in exceptional circumstances. In those circumstances, there is a companion thought: Why should I make this specific individual an example to the rest of our society? Does this individual deserve to be so used by society? More often than not, the response is a clear NO!

We should keep things in the proper perspective. The above discussion does not mean that jails should be torn down or that specific individuals should not be sent to spend time in jail. No, there is no doubt that society has the right to be protected from specific individuals. If an individual cannot freely roam our streets without threatening society, that individual's freedom should be curtailed. The next question is how much should that freedom be curtailed? If that freedom is completely curtailed, then the issue is in what kind of habitat should that person be placed?

A judge who decides that complete limitation of the individual's freedom will serve no legitimate interest can place that person on probation or in a program such as work release. A person on probation or in a work release program, is not completely free. That person must be supervised by a arm of society: the probation officer.

In deciding how much of an individual's freedom should be limited, a judge must determine the needs of that individual and of society. The judge must also determine what the individual and society have to offer each other.

There are times when a judge believes that incarcerating a person will not benefit anyone in the long range. But can the judge place a person on probation if he believes that probation will fail because society has not allocated enough resources to rehabilitate offenders? A judge may face an individual who has been convicted for the crime of drawing checks on insufficient funds. The primary reason for that person's behavior may have been economic need or inability to obtain work because of the economy or the lack of skills. It may be that the individual cannot retain a job because of complex emotional problems.

Sending that individual to jail will benefit no one. But can a judge allow that person to continue writing checks at the expense of society? What a judge would like to do in situations like that is to place the offender in a program which will help solve the offender's problems; such a program may involve training to acquire new skills, help in obtaining a job, or attention and cure of the offender's emotional problems.

While there are *some* programs that a judge may use, very commonly the existing programs are so understaffed and their resources are so limited that placing an offender in such a program is nothing more than to set that person up for another failure in life. The program (and therefore society) will fail the offender because of the lack of resources, and the offender will probably fail society again in the future. As a result, a judge sometimes sends a person to jail not because incarceration is the best answer, but because there is no other possible alternative.

Another problem that a judge must face as a result of under-staffing and lack of resources in this kind of program is that even if a judge decides to take a chance with an individual of-fender, expecting that the program will not fail again, the judge subconsciously will realize that perhaps another offender already in the program will be hurt with the addition of another person to share the limited resources.

We must, however, face reality. Not every offender can be placed on probation or in a work release program. For the best interests of the individual and of society, offenders must some-times be completely restrained from roaming in our streets.

In completely restraining an individual, we must be aware of the choices. We could on one hand send that individual to Sun Valley, Lake Tahoe or the Carribean. The individual would not be able to leave the area, and would have to spend the sen-tence basking in the sun or practicing some new skiing tech-niques. On the other hand, we could send the individual to a place where the individual would be chained to a wall for the entire period of the sentence. Both choices sound, and are, im-practical in that they would not help achieve any of society's goals. But if those choices are so impractical, why do we seem to stick so closely, in reality if not in theory, to the second choice?

It may be argued that our prisons do not resemble the second choice. I would disagree.

I spent twenty hours once in the Nevada State Penitentiary as part of the program of the State Trial Judge College in Reno, Nevada. I was allegedly busted for carrying contraband, and remember very clearly my entry into institutional life. I was first placed in the Maximum Security Facility where, together with my companions, we were processed through mugging, finger-printing, showering and delousing. After all that, which seemed to take an eternity, but actually only took a couple of hours, we were transferred to the Medium Security Facility.

One of the first impressions I gained of prison life was the fact that convicts have their own alien, but fully developed, society; their own traditions and customs; their perculiar caste, system;

and a code of conduct more solid than that practiced by free men. In my opinion, most of those convicts were simply doing their time, not being rehabilitated, and their social order was designated to make this process bearable.

Lack of activity, lack of a program, and lack of meaningful work appeared to be a major gripe of the inmates.

Another thing that immediately struck me was the curse of racism which was induced by the self-segregation of whites, blacks and Indians. I was told that each group had their own areas where nonmembers would not dare to wander.

It was very interesting that I, an innocent person, immediately felt that the inmates, guilty or innocent, were my peers! The guards, without doubt, were the opposition, not a part of our make-believe society, and not to be trusted. That was the tacit imperative of the system, and it is uncanny how swiftly and how instinctively it was absorbed by our group of innocent men, if not by clairvoyance at least by osmosis! The tabu would be enforced by ostracism, and worse, by violence if necessary. A man would have to make it with his peers, whether he liked it or not, and he could not seek the intervention of the authorities when threatened, or his days of living in this subculture society would end. Sad as it may be, we not only place prisoners in inhuman exile from our society, but we also arrange, or allow things to be, so that they live in their own little nations which are at war with each other, with society, and with the penal authorities.

The concept of iron resistance to the penal system was further enforced by the psychodrama that we observed. The new inmate, or *fish*, receives an introduction to prison life, in spite of penal authorities, that makes the old fashioned fraternity pledging a kind of gentle practice. I got, in my brief visit, the impression that in prison the wrong response can be a form of suicide. While twenty hours in jail do not make me an expert, it was an experience that has made me think a great deal about the purgatory to which I sent some offenders.

What does all this say about you, me, and more importantly, our society?

The advent of penitentiaries in the early days of our republic was, at the time, a great advance in penology. Before that, felons were sentenced to be branded, burned, or simply executed. The humanitarians of that era prompted incarceration as a progressive alternative to inhuman physical abuses.

The Quakers thereafter came forth with the idea of solitary confinement to bring about a penitent state of mind. Insanity and death often followed. Only the extraordinarily strong, of mind and physique, could endure the solitary confinement. This type of incarceration was replaced by the Auburn System of rigid discpline, hard labor, utter silence, shaved heads, lock-step marching, and slavish toil in huge isolated cages.

I cannot put my finger on it, but there is something to be learned by a society that had to wait for James Cagney, Paul Muni and Wallace Berry to give us our first impressions of the *Big House* and this system of incarceration.

Who is to blame for our present state of affairs? Society, without doubt! But we must never forget the elements of society: you and I! Students, physicians, lawyers, psychologists, penal authorities, legislators, judges and the like. As individuals, we lay the issue aside by blaming society. Instead, we must act in a more realistic capacity.

It has been said that the judiciary's *Hands Off Policy* is a product of judicial deference to putative administrative expertise, but whatever the theory, it has almost prevented significant judicial inquiry into the administration of penal institutions. Other professions, besides the judiciary, have their own excuses for not having worked actively toward necessary reforms.

Inactivity by those who should be active has developed a gap between the courts, other professionals and the prison authorities. Such a gap would not normally be allowed by society, or by us, in any other substantial aspect of life. Nevertheless, in the field of penology we allow such a gap to exist as a matter of course.

In defense of the courts, it should be pointed out that many courts have actively done their share to improve our penal system. Some of those courts have had a great impact in our legal and nonlegal thinking. First there was the case of *Weems vs. United States*, 217 US 349 (1910) in which the Eighth Amendment was invoked against a sentence to "hard and painful labor." By dictum the opinion indicated that the application of the Eighth Amendment should not be limited only to physical brutality towards prisoners, but may have a vague but broader meaning as public opinion became more enlightened.

For almost sixty years, jurisprudence languished serenely without prodding by either society or those directly involved with the prison system. In 1968, however, the courts finally dealt directly with the nonphysical aspects of punishment in *Jackson vs. Bishop,* 404 F2d 571.

In the Jackson case, the court cited both physical brutality and lack of rehabilitative potential as relevant factors in condemning the use of the whip under the protection of the Eighth Amendment. In addition, the convict in that case successfully asserted a substantive claim for freedom from the infliction of "cruel and unusual punishment" in the context of what the court regarded to be a "class action."

Because of the acceptance of the "class action" concept, the Jackson case offered the prospect of facilitating the review of general prison conditions, such as lack of rehabilitative protections, by expanding the scope of prison experiences which a court may consider relevant.

Unfortunately, the Jackson case merely hinted that lack of rehabilitative treatment could stand alone as a factor and in the court's opinion lack of such care was intertwined with the traditional concept of physical brutality under the Eighth Amendment.

In *Sostre vs. McGinnis,* 334 F2d 906, a 1964 decision, the Second Circuit considered the constitutionality of solitary confinement in excess of fifteen days.

Although the court was unwilling to condemn such treatment as cruel and unusual merely because it found it to be "personally repugnant," the court did announce *objective sources* upon which a cruel and unusual finding might be based: (1) historic usage (2) practices in other jurisdictions (3) public opinion. The court then decided not to condemn Sostre's treatment as cruel and unusual, largely due to the prevalence of similar practices in other jurisdictions.

Under the Second Circuit's approach, as progressively more

states begin to experiment with programs for rehabilitation, the lack of such programs could come to constitute cruel and unusual punishment.

As this movement to shrink the limits of physical brutality has gained momentum, courts have begun gradually to recognize the need to expand the prohibition of cruel and unusual punishment into the area of psychological cruelty and personality damage.

The most important of these decisions was *Holt vs. Sarver*, 307 F Supp 362 (1970) which declared in a class action that the entire Arkansas Penitentiary System, as then operated, constituted cruel and unusual punishment. It was the condemnation of a whole environment corrupted by medieval malice and by outrages both physical and spiritual. In so sweeping a challenge, the court discarded the odd but traditional distinction between assaults upon the body and the ruin of the life and spirit.

As it may be remembered from the news stories of the investigation, the Arkansas system consisted of two work farms where inmates supposedly labored in the fields raising agricultural products to be sold for the benefit of the state. In reality, inmate labor was often contracted out to personal friends of the warden and members of the parole board and the inmates were forced to work on projects returning no revenue to the state.

The system offered no program of rehabilitation and made no attempt to prepare the inmates for release.

The system did not even employ correctional workers, but instead it used armed inmate *trustees* who were often used to guard other inmates. No overt efforts were made to protect the inmates from possible assaults. The most devastating disclosure in that incident was the discovery of inmates' skeletons in a presumably fertile field.

The Holt decision is important in three respects:

First, it recognized that the lack of a meaningful program of rehabilitation is significant in adjudging punishment to be cruel and unusual.

The court in Holt even implied that the lack of a meaningful rehabilitation program could eventually and conceivably become an independent constitutional basis for defining cruel and unusual punishment. The court observed that many sociological themes and ideas "had ripened" into constitutional significance within society in general, but that the rehabilitation of convicts had not yet achieved this decisive stature.

The court thus recognized that social necessity can raise, to constitutionally protected status, factors which previously were not so enshrined.

Although the judiciary seems to be on the brink of a major breakthrough in the area of prison reforms, there are several factors which severely inhibit the potential of judiciary intervention.

One is the most direct limitation, the one that restricts the relief which the judiciary can grant. We do not control the purse strings, nor can we command the legislators to appropriate funds.

Second, the very nature of judicial proceedings, within the common-law tradition of isolated narrow issues and adversary argument, is not ideally suited to develop workable blueprints for prison reform. The protagonist argues for confinement as it exists, the antagonist cries for freedom. The opition available to the court has two sides and no middle.

Third is the evident lack of judicial expertise in penology.

The burden of supervising and enforcing any systematic and practical curative program may overly burden the judicial process. Someone else must be our brother's keeper, we can only consign him to the keeping, unless our numbers and our opportunities are expanded.

In spite of all these problems blocking judicial intervention, some kind of supervision of a flexible and decisive nature, essentially judicial and at least judicious, cannot and should not be forever postponed. If the legislatures, the correctional authorities, and the executive branches of government permit intolerable conditions to exist; when human neglect and indifference causes human beings to be treated as slaves left to rot and ferment in social warehouses, the courts, simply because they have the power to be inventive and humane, must act. Otherwise, the remedy is in the province of parole boards, acting after misery has achieved its tragic spoil; too late and too variable to be a real avenue for correction.

If rehabilitation is to be the goal of modern corrections, then we must practice what we preach. Just as judges have the power to imprison certainly judges have the power to try to salvage. If the penitentiaries cannot physically provide real correction, if they are simple morgues for the civilly dead, we will have to decide some better method of dealing with those convicts who could become useful men again, given an opportunity better than dismal decay.

As I have stated above, the judges have done something to improve our penal systems. But as I have also stated, we judges as a group have not done enough. Having placed myself and my judicial brothers on the spot, now I do not hesitate in pointing out that many others involved in our prison system are on the spot, too. They, as we judges, should not try to escape. Instead we should unite in an effort to either improve, or as some critics have said, discard our present prison system.

The humanitarians of our era must come forward with a better alternative to our present system of incarceration. While our present system is better than the one we had in times past when we mutilated, burned, and killed offenders, our present system is not good enough for our society. We must all come together, pool our resources, and establish a better system. We owe that not only to ourselves, but to each other and to society. We must look forward to the day when a judge, without doing injustice to the offender or society, may finish the statement

". . . therefore, I hereby sentence you to . . ."

CHAPTER IV

WE HAVE FAILED IN OUR EFFORTS TO REHABILITATE THE RECIDIVIST BURGLAR

MYRON WARREN

IN 1964 FBI Uniform Crime Reports Releases show that over 1,100,000 of the more than 2,600,000 serious crimes committed in the U.S. were burglaries; that is close to one-half the total crime.

A 1964 Utah prison official's survey revealed that approximately one-fourth of the penitentiary population, the largest single criminal group, was serving time for some variation of the state burglary statutes. These are staggering figures indeed. I believe they were aided in their climb by two U.S. Supreme Court decisions: (a) *Escobedo vs. Illinois* (1964) and (b) *Miranda vs. Arizona* (1966). These two decisions have had a great effect on law enforcement, particularly burglary investigations. State courts throughout the U.S. use these two rulings as guide lines in their decision making. The resulting decisions, in many instances, restrict the law enforcement officer in his efforts against crime.

Mention must also be made of the Bail Reform Act of 1966. This act was an outgrowth of a study made in New York City by the Vera Institute. This project endeavored to study the results of handling individuals kept in jail on minor charges, especially traffic violations. Between the years of 1961 and 1964, the courts released 3,500 persons without bail into the project. Surprisingly enough, fifty individuals failed to return to court. This is a very good program for what it was designed. The intent of the 1966

Bail Reform Act was not to permissively release, time and again, individuals charged with felony offenses before bringing them to trial. Courts have, however, used the Vera Institute philosophy by returning to society many burglars prior to trial and without posting bail.

The Escobedo and Miranda decisions, coupled with the Bail Reform Act enable a burglar to remain on the streets for months, even years, before being brought to trial. The habitual burglar can by this means repeat his crime while enjoying his freedom.

In addition to the above, a new phenomenon has recently occurred. The female burglar was not a common figure in the past; but since the spread of drug useage among juveniles, more females are involved in burglaries. Many youths today, with no previous arrest record, have found it necessary to support their drug habit by a career in burglary.

Another factor contributing to the rising burglary rate is the permissiveness of some rehabilitation programs.

Most burglars begin their careers in crime when they are young, stealing small items around the neighborhood and graduating to *Big Time* as their needs develop. This gives the recidivist (habitual) burglar a long time to add to the staggering figures we are considering.

The 1969 FBI Reports state that burglaries have increased 117 percent, while law enforcement agencies solve less than one out of every five burglaries. This appalling increase is occurring, in part, because the criminal justice system has failed in their efforts to rehabilitate the recidivist burglar.

If the people in the criminal justice system are going to reverse these rising crime figures, the criminals basic character must be understood. Three major mistakes have occurred in efforts to understand the characteristics of the recidivist burglar: 1. We erroneously assume that no one chooses to be a burglar of his own free will. We seldom consider the free choice between right and wrong; the free choice of action each burglar has had from the very beginning of his career in crime. 2. We place too much blame on society for the burglars' failure to accept rehabilitation. 3. We have failed to study the thrill aspect of his criminal habits.

I consider the thrill aspect of the recidivist burglar as the dominant factor in his habitual life of crime. I have conducted hundreds of interviews with recidivist burglars; the common denominator—thrill and excitement were *always* present. There are two general types of burglars, the professional and the amateur. Some professionals make their living by burglary alone and have no other income; while others may maintain full time employment as a cover-up for their burglary activities. The rest are amateurs.

In the professional group, and at the top of the list are the safe burglars—included in this group is the professional recidivist. The burglar, who is in and out of prison, and returns to the crime of burglary because this type of crime holds the greatest amount of excitement and thrill.

Partial justification for this opinion can be seen from the following tape recorded interviews:

> To me it was always the excitement more than the money. I never felt bad if there wasn't money. The most exciting part was going in, the entry, you know, going in there in the dark, when you didn't know for sure what was waiting. Oh man! Opening the safe, I would sweat so hard my clothes would be wringing wet, just as if I had done a day's work.

Another burglar described the thrill of running ahead of the watchman in a dark warehouse and hiding. And how, on another occasion, he lay with his heart pounding, in a snowbank, as a policeman sought him with a flashlight and pistol:

> It's something like being a dope addict, it gets in your blood. I first got the feeling when I was a kid and burglarized the grade school. Then I broke into the Grange Hall. After that I never quit.

A third burglar stated that on one occasion it took him at least two hours to make an entry into a store. He cut out a section large enough to permit him to enter, by drilling a series of holes, one overlapping the other. As he expressed it:

> 90 percent of the excitement was experienced during the two hours it took to drill out the section.

He would turn the brace one turn at a time, as the bit ground into the wood making a harsh sound in the stillness, it would send chills through his entire body. He would stop and listen to learn if anyone had observed him. After he dropped into the store, if he couldn't find money in a twenty minute search, he had to leave because he became so unnerved he would start to shake. It took him hours after he reached home to quiet down.

A fourth burglar related,

> I started prowling at the age of fourteen years just for the thrill. Once I made up my mind I was going on a particular night, the tension would start and the excitement would seep in. I'd drive to the scene, always using the back roads and streets to avoid any contact with prowl cars. I would gradually become more *geared-up* as I approached the crime scene. The point of entry was always the peak of tension. If I happened to be *ranked-off* the job by officers checking the building, I would really reach an extreme peak of tension. My adrenalin would be pumping to such a degree that I could clear a six foot fence with ease, to escape the scene. A close brush with the officers was always the most extreme type of excitement.

Another burglar called *The Shovel Burglar* because he usually used a shovel to pry open windows, was an early evening prowler. After one of his arrests, he *cleared* approximately four hundred house burglaries which he committed in Oregon, Washington, and Idaho. He was a commercial fisherman, and he claimed that during the fishing season, he had a few problems with burglary; but when the season was over, he would return to the city. Each evening as it started to get dark and he finished his evening meal, the urge to go out and prowl became unbearable. He would pace the floor and smoke one cigarette after another and argue with himself that he should not go, because the law of averages was going to catch up with him. He said he never won one of these arguments—he always went. He would drive into a neighborhood seeking a home to prowl, one with the lights out, where he felt the occupants were out for the evening. He used the same procedures as most house burglars use prior to entry, that is: ring the front door bell, if no one answered, walked around to the back door and try there. When he was reasonably sure no one was home, he would go to the garage or some outside storage area in search of a shovel to pry open a window. When he entered, climbing over the windowsill, would bring on the peak of tension. Once inside, if he was unable to find any money within twenty to twenty-five minutes, he would become so unnerved that any noise from the outside would cause him to leave. He said on several occasions he got the *shakes* when he was *flushed* from a house by the arrival of the police. He would always hide in the darkness, never far from the scene and try to conceal himself from the searching police. There were occasions when the police brushed close by him, and this was always the time of greatest excitement. He, like the others, in order to gain complete emotional satisfaction in one evening, would prowl from one to three houses. This generally is considered the emotional limit for the average burglar.

It is difficult for most people, as well as some policemen, to understand how the excitement and thrill of planning and execution of the plan totally involves the recidivist burglar. The following excerpts taken from an interview will help illustrate these points.

This interview was conducted with Hubert, a residential burglar. At the time of the interview, Hubert was thirty-six years of age and waiting to be sentenced on the charge of residential burglary in Oregon; had served time in a Florida Chain Gang and San Quentin Penitentiary for residential burglaries.

Hubert admitted to committing more than one hundred house burglaries in the Metropolitan area of Portland.

THE INTERVIEW

W: Would you give a little background on your personal life as to your younger years? What kind of home life did you have?

H: There wasn't a great deal of home life. I was one of four children. My father worked for the railroad. My parents had quite a drinking problem when they were younger. I was the only redhead in the family and when anything ever happened, "Red did it". When I was quite young, I started running away from home and consequently I ended up in Elroy State Training School for Boys, for eighteen months.

W: What age were you?

H: I was twelve, maybe thirteen at that time.

W: What age were you when you got into trouble with the law, other than running away from home?

H: It was in 1946, when I burglarized three homes and was caught for the burglary and consequently given three years in a Florida Chain Gang.

W: How old were you at the time?

H: I was nineteen at that time.

W: Had you any previous criminal record such as stealing, minor thefts?

H: Not actually, I had taken things before, but not in the sense that they were outright crimes, they were things that most children do like, stealing milk bottles and trading them in for the money, and stuff like that.

W: How old were you when you stole the first time?

H: I'm afraid I can't remember that far back.

W: Were you in grade school or high school?

H: I'm sure it was in grade school.

W: What was your next arrest?

H: It was about three months after I got out of the chain gang, I came here to Portland, Oregon, and was arrested here for the same type of crime.

W: House burglary?

H: That's right.

W: And the one that followed that?

H: The one that followed that was in California, wait, no, the one that followed was in Canada.

W: And what was that?

H: That was the church burglary.

W: That's the only other burglary that you have against you that isn't house burglary?

H: That's right.

W: Then, the next one is . . .

H: In California.

W: And that's for house burglary?

H: That's right.

W: Where did you do your time?

H: I went to San Quentin for the first twenty-two months of my sentence and for the last eight months, I went to another institution.

W: Were you released, or did you receive a parole?

H: I was placed on a two and a half year parole.

W: Did you do your parole?

H: Yes, I did.

W: Did you steal while on parole?

H: No, I didn't.

W: Your present arrest is the one following San Quentin, your arrest here in Washington County?

H: That's right, yes.

W: You have cleaned up about one hundred house burglaries in the general area of Portland, the Metropolitan area, which includes parts of Clackamas, Multnomah counties, the City of Portland, and Washington County.

H: Yes.

W: And at the present time, you're waiting trial?

H: I'm waiting for sentencing now.

W: You plead guilty?

H: I plead guilty.

W: Let's start with the type of houses you select.

H: I'd say, generally, it was a middle class or medium type house.

W: Why?

H: I felt that the lower class homes didn't have anything of any consequence that would be of any value and the higher class homes would have things of value but I would have no means of disposing of them, or I thought that I hadn't; so I got into the habit of going to the middle class or the executive type home, generally a junior executive type home, where as I felt there was a possibility of cash or the type of jewelry that I might be able to get rid of.

W: Was there any particular basis on how you selected your homes in the medium class group?

H: Generally speaking, I picked the homes in a general area, where I felt that possibly I had the better chance of getting what I wanted. Of course, I always tried to choose a home where there was a little foliage or shrubbery or something around the house, where as I wouldn't be too easily disturbed or bothered getting into a home. I tried, as best I could, to find one that had an easy entry, such as sliding doors and the like. I never chose a home which I had cased.

W: You didn't pick a house that you had cased?

H: Very seldom did I ever do this.

W: You drove into the area and then picked out a house as you were driving around?

H: No. On a couple of instances, I had found names and addresses in the society section of the newspaper where I felt that these people would be away from home on a particular evening, and consequently, I might go by the house prior to the particular date and look the house over and try to find anything that would indicate that there were children in the house or other people. I would come back on the night in question, or call prior to my coming back in the area. If there was no answer to my phone call, I would come back and go into the house. But, ordinarily, my method of picking a particular house was more or less knowing the area which I was going into and driving around that particular area and finding a house that I felt at the time might be vacated by people at the present and then proceed to determine whether there was anyone at home, and if not I would go ahead and break in.

W: How did you ascertain from the ad in the paper what was suitable for you?

H: Well, ordinarily, I would scan the society sheet and it would tell about an upcoming party or an upcoming wedding or reception or something of that type. There were the names of the people that were in charge of these particular functions. I felt almost assured that if there weren't any small children or other people living in the house, that this would be possibly a good time to try.

W: You were trying to avoid contact in a home where there were small children, is this right?

H: That's right.

W: Why is this?

H: Well, ordinarily, if they had children, they had babysitters. I wanted no part of a home that had anyone in it anyway for the simple reason that this is a dangerous situation.

W: If someone happend to be there, what would you do, did you have any excuse for being there?

H: I always felt that if someone were to come to the door, I could ask for some fictitious person that I thought was in this particular neighborhood and ask if they were this particular individual, and if they weren't, I would ask them if they knew the whereabouts of a street in the general area that I knew was there.

W: Were there certain days of the week that you preferred?

H: Very definitely. Friday and Saturday were the better nights for this type of burglarizing.

W: Did you generally confine your burglary to these two nights?

H: That's right.

W: How about the time of night?

H: It may generally between dusk and ten, maybe ten-thirty P.M.

W: Any particular reason for this?

H: This would be the general time that they would be out and there would be less chance of being caught in the premises or being startled out of it.

W: Was there any precautions the home owner might have taken which would stop you?

H: There were two or three things. The presence of a large dog loose in the house. Second, an electric light in a particular part of the house where as I couldn't be sure whether there were anyone in a room or not. Third, a radio or a TV playing in the house.

W: What's the best place to have a light?

H: I think the best place would be either the bathroom or the bedroom.

W: Why do you say this?

H: If someone's in the bath, they might not be able to come to the door—or couldn't hear.

W: You mentioned earlier about how you selected houses with sliding doors.

H: That patio type door.

W: Did you generally carry a tool?

H: I carried a large screw driver and nothing more.

W: How did you use it?

H: Ordinarily there is a little space between the door and the doorjam. I got close to the locking mechanism and put a little pressure on it, and consequently it forced it open.

W: What can a home owner do to protect this particular type of door?

H: The simplist thing I would suggest is to put a board or mop handle or anything that had been cut to size, down in the bottom sliding section of the door, it would be quite difficult to make an entry without making a lot of noise or even breaking the glass or taking the door off it's sliding deal completely.

W: What's the first thing you do when you get inside?

H: Ordinarily, I make it a point to stand inside the door and determine by noises whether anyone had observed me going into the house. If I felt they had, they would probably come around to part of the house to check for themselves.

W: How long would it take you?

H: I'd just stay there momentarily to satisfy myself. I didn't want to stay in the house any longer than I had to.

W: What was your next move?

H: I went completely through the house to make sure that there wasn't anyone in the house at all.

W: What kind of light would you use?

H: I used a medium sized flashlight.

W: You wouldn't turn the lights on in the house?

H: No, sir.

W: Have you ever encountered a dog in the house?

H: If the dog hadn't started acting up prior to my getting into the house I got the impression that the dog wasn't too violent, I would put him in a room, and lock him in.

W: Have you ever found anyone asleep in the house?

H: Only once, and that was several years ago.

W: How far would you park your car away from the house you prowled?

H: That depended on how light the area was. If it was a well-lit area, I parked at least a block away, and sometimes even farther. If it weren't too well lit. I parked it at least a half a block away. I never parked too close to a house.

W: Would you park in any particular place in the block?

H: Ordinarily I tried to find a place where I wouldn't be boxed in, where I could get out readily, on the corner.

W: No one could park in front of you.

H: That's right.

W: So you could get away fast.

H: Right.

W: The automobile that you used, was it your own car?

H: Yes, it was.

W: Registered to you?

H: That's right.

W: Where did you carry your tools?

H: Under the front seat: I had a flashlight, a screw driver and a pair of gloves.

W: What if a policeman stopped you on the way to a burglary and saw underneath the seat that you had a screw driver, gloves, and a flashlight, what would your answer be to the policeman?

H: Well, I was pretty well dressed, I generally wore a suit and a tie and white shirt. I would tell them that I had either just had difficulty with the car and I wore the gloves so that I wouldn't get dirty. The flashlight, of course, was to see what I was fooling with and the screw driver was to test and see if I was getting spark from my spark plugs or tightening a bolt or screw or something under the hood.

W: Why would you dress up in a suit?

H: Well, with a suit, there was less chance of being suspicioned. If I were a policeman and I saw a person in a suit in an area where there had been a burglary committed I certainly wouldn't be looking for someone in a business suit with adequate money, or with a diamond ring I used to wear. It just didn't seem quite the thing to stop someone like this when you were looking for a burglar.

W: You would wear a diamond ring?

H: Yes.

W: How many houses did you break into in one night?

H: Not more than three.

W: Would you go directly home?

H: Yes.

W: When you arrived at home, what would you do?

H: I would leave it in the car or place it somewhere in the garage, where it would be out of sight. If it was groceries, of course, I would take them in the house and place them in the refrigerator. Sometimes I would proceed into the house, probably the bathroom and turn the light on and check what I had. If it were something that I didn't feel that I wanted in the house, then I would go out and put it back into the car or put it into the garage until I got rid of it.

W: Do you ever have any feeling, sensation of excitement or thrill, in burglarizing a place?

H: Every time.

W: Do you think you were aware of this when you started prowling years ago?

H   No, I don't believe that I was. I realized that there was a great deal of fear involved and a great deal of excitment, quite a let down afterwards, but it never impressed me as anything but fear of doing something wrong and being apprehended for it.

W: This fear, this excitement, is present in all burglaries? When do you first feel this sensation?

H: When I first decide whether it's ten hours before or two or three days before, when I actually make up my mind that I intend to do something on a particular day. At that moment, I have a momentary feeling of fear and apprehension. Of course, the day I pull the burglary, why certainly prior to leaving the house, this is certainly a time of great apprehension to me.

W: As soon as you decided "I'm going to go", this is when this apprehension or this fear, this enthusiasm, or whatever it might be, starts to become a part of you? Do you have any arguments with yourself, as to the right and wrong?

H: I'm sure that I do, yes, I don't think that there has been anytime that I can remember where I didn't feel that this was very definitely a wrong situation, but I let my lesser judgement rule my better judgement and consequently the fact that I probably am quite lazy and I don't care to get out and work, or to ask for help from other sources. My feeling of melancholy and thinking that things weren't going quite right for me, and that this was the only out.

W: Let's say that you've been working for several months and not doing any stealing. You decide to go back to stealing—does it come easier then?

H: I think it's quite difficult to get started again.

W: Once you have started, then is it easier?

H: It's a regular process, it's just a matter of gaining momentum and picking up and going from there. After I pull a couple of burglaries and they have been successful, it's quite easy.

SECTION THREE
WITHIN THE WALLS

CHAPTER V

PRACTICAL CONSIDERATIONS ON PRISON ADMINISTRATION OF TREATMENT PROGRAMS

WILLIAM HOFFSTETTER

THIS CHAPTER WILL not deal with the notions that correctional rehabilitation programs have historically been disastrous or the uptopian concept that there is a perfect system somewhere waiting to be discovered. I will, however, be working with some of the real *here and now* aspects of correctional systems management that are presently in operation in several penal facilities.

It has been my experience based on twenty years of juvenile and adult correctional work, both as a clinical psychologist and program administrator, that two consistent elements emerge.

One factor suggests that whenever a group of offenders are interacting, that interaction has structure and is systematic. Whether or not the system is directed toward the offender's rehabilitation or towards accelerating his criminal behavior depends largely on the expertise of the administrator to guide the system in a positive direction.

The second factor is that the more an inmate is involved in his own rehabilitation process the more effective will be the outcome. A report by the United States President's Commission on Law Enforcement and Administration of Justice states, "Inmate inducement in institution management groups can thus be still another mechanism, in addition to those already described, for reducing the extent to which prison social structure alienates

53

inmates from noncriminal persons and increases their identification with the offender."

Generally, the participation of inmates in the administration of adult and juvenile programs has not worked.

Either they have tended to be almost totally controlled by institutional personnel or they have been taken over by the *cons.*

A clear definition at the beginning of the process to involve inmate participation is of critical importance. Participation must be spelled out in precise terms regarding the extent of the authority, power, direction and limitations of each participant, as well as the group as a whole.

I was the Associate Director of a rather innovative program in one of the large penitentiaries on the west coast whose goal was to encourage and provide selected inmates with the necessary resources to complete college. The plan was to offer sufficient college level courses in the institutions to assist the inmate to adjust to the necessary learning and social tasks that would confront them at an *outside university,* and upon release enroll and hopefully complete a bachelor's degree program.

The program began without stress but as the participants began *opting* for involvement (what one would expect in a *regular* university), it became evident that the program did not have clear guidelines for dealing with this kind of problem. In fact, the program quickly took on the flavor of San Francisco State College at its highlight, with the *cons,* pressuring for more freedom, which essentially meant a request of a *taking over* program. As a result the program was in serious trouble.

Much of this could have been prevented if early in the process, the perameters of the extent of inmate government were laid down with the convict's consent.

Later, I had better results when, as Director of the Diagnostic Center for a large first-felony institution, we decided to establish an inmate housing unit that operated without direction from the administration. The inmates were to have control over the unit which would in fact help them experience and be aware of the problems of self-government. It would also give the staff some concrete notion of the inmates' ability or inability to deal with many of the factors necessary for survival outside of the institution. Needless to say, this program involved a great deal of risk-taking by the superintendent.

Recalling some of our previous errors of not involving inmates in the planning process, we allowed for sufficient time for everyone to know what was happening. We kept the total inmate population informed of the progress through news letters and discussion groups. Actually, the total inmate group was aware of what was being accomplished and as a result they were in support of the principles of limited self-government.

This program has been in successful operation for five years and was the model for many similar programs around the nation.

As the effectiveness of involving inmates into the administration of institutional programs began to show results, disciplinary reports reduced in numbers and severity—there were less assaultive-aggressive behaviors—and a general overall improvement in climate between inmate and staff, particularly with the correctional officers.

We felt it necessary to reinforce this kind of interaction and sought ways to bring this into being. We felt with a great deal of certitude that many inmates reacted negatively to the correctional officer's uniform, rather than to the officer as a person. In other words, the uniform represented a barrier which hindered the inmate from perceiving the officer in his *humanness.* The uniform became a symbol which created distance and alienation on the officers part. We saw the uniform as serving no positive rehabilitative function in the institution and we took steps to bring about its disuse.

Accepting the notion that inmates respond more appropriately if included in the planning phases, we used this same concept in our planning operation to eliminate uniforms.

We presented the idea to the correctional officer group and asked for their ideas. Many of the officer's were in support of eliminating uniforms. These officers did suggest some problems. For instance, officers were compensated for their notoriously low pay be being furnished uniforms and dry cleaning, at public expense. After some negotiation, it was decided that the state would furnish the first set of *civilian clothes* and that replacements would be made by officers. Dry cleaning would be state furnished and a successful attempt was made to increase the officer's salary to cover cost of replacing clothing.

The elimination of uniforms resulted in lessening of tension, alienation and hostility between *guard* and *con* and has tended to facilitate a healthier rapport. In other words, the behavioral message is now, *I want to help you as a person,* rather than, *I want you to keep your distance, since I am here to discipline you.*

Initiating rehabilitation programs in correctional facilities generally meets with resistance at various levels and administrators should be prepared to deal with this resistance. Such comments can be expected from staff as, "Jails are no place to do treatment." The most vigorous hue and cry is, "We don't have time to rehabilitate."

One of the processes in the facility that frustrated both inmates and staff was the pass system. Inmates were issued passes by the officer whenever they moved around the institution, much as a *hall pass* is used in many of our high schools today. It required much of the officer's time to deal with the filling-in, stamping, and monitoring of this process which seemed again to serve little purpose outside of treating the *con* like a child, thereby reinforcing his dependency needs.

After some discussion with the warden, it was decided to try, for a period of time, to go without the pass system. The feedback from staff and inmates was so overwhelming in support of what happened that the warden allowed us to use the time saved to establish a group therapy program.

I have attempted to describe some of the methods which can be more rehabilitative in our penal institutions.

Involving the staff and particularly the *cons* in the planning and programming process is vital to the process of any rehabilitative effort. I recently attended a lecture by Dr. Carl Rogers who also felt that clients make progress in the group to a greater extent when they are involved in what is happening to them.

Innovative program administrators can expect a good deal of resistance from both staff and inmates; particularly the, *We don't have time to rehabilitate* game. It will be up to the program planner to create ways to meet those resistances by eliminating those counter productive processes such as uniforms and pass systems.

CHAPTER VI

THE CORRECTIONAL COUNSELOR AS A CHANGE AGENT

Roger D. Owen

I T HAS LONG been the writer's position that anyone deriving his livelihood from the presence of a social or physical malady, whether individual or group, should work at the same time for the amelioration of the condition. It can be observed that a basic phenomenon of bureaucracy is that gradually the institution begins to exist primarily for its perpetuation. Other considerations, including the institution's ostensible purpose soon become contingent upon this criterion. Thus, only in working toward prevention, as well as rehabilitation, can an individual employed in such a setting be possibly in a morally tenable position, according to this writer.

It is my assumption that my position holds true for a variety of professional people. For instance, it is valid for the heart specialist who does no research. It applies to the vice squad officer, who does not attempt to eliminate the need individuals and groups have that cause them to prey upon one another. It also applies to the corrections worker at any level in the system, who is not trying his utmost to alter in some may the conditions within society that create and maintain prisons.

Another value-premise pertinent to this chapter affirms that the counselor has certain moral imperatives entrusted to him by the very definition of the term counseling, i.e., by his role defi-

57

nition. [The correctional counselor must work both within the correctional setting and in the larger community to identify and work toward those ends which will cause the early demise of prisons, as we know them.]

In the correctional setting, typical counseling goals are defeated by the preclusion of the conditions for treatment. They are: (1) the absence of a climate of trust; (2) mutual respect for people; and (3) the options necessary to carry out a viable treatment program for the individual inmate.

Before examining at greater length the correctional counselor's current role, it is necessary to review some of the dysfunctional aspects of penal institutions. The ideas which are the subject of this chapter are the conclusions which follow these assumptions concerning the structure of our prisons.

At the outset of incarceration, a peculiar process ensues. The newly arrived inmate finds his reality sharply curtailed and his self-defining mechanisms limited to a few options. The guards and staff, in an effort to accomplish a variety of goals, one of which is to uniformly process him from his civilian role to that of inmate. Goffman (1961) terms this mortification; perhaps a more appropriate term is *dehumanization.*

[The counselor has a critical role in the process. These effects stem largely from the process already referred to as dehumanization.] Its three cardinal aspects are:

1. Changes due to adjustment in prison life.
2. Changes due to loss of contact with the outside world.
3. Changes due to deterioration.

In the wake of Attica, it has been noted that prison represents the perfect bureaucracy, as Shrag (1971) notes in his article.

The counselor, as well as the remainder of the staff, foster and aid in the maintenance of the inmate subculture by initiating the mortification power over the lives of the captive group. Until quite recently, no attempts to alter this condition have been made. The maxim, ("Keep things running smoothly") appears to be the principle value.

PRISONER POWER: A NEW CONSIDERATION
Until recently, the public, the courts, the press, and the civil

rights groups, etc., were unable to penetrate the unscrutability of the prison. Said a bit differently, convicts couldn't get out, and others couldn't get in. Jessica Mitford (1970) states, "Prisons are traditionally secret places, hermetically sealed off from public and judicial scrutiny." As a result of some recent changes, the public, through exposure in the media, and the courts perhaps for the same reason, are beginning to show more concern for inmate life.

Changes in the status quo seemingly rest on the convergence of three primary factors. First, there is a rise in militancy and change in the *poor me* self-concept toward one of increasing dignity in an evergrowing number of inmates, as a result of the Black Muslim Movement, beginning to assert influence in U.S. prisons in the early 1960's, and more recently in the advent of the Black Panthers and similar groups.

Secondly, the incarceration of the more sophisticated offender, who may be a conscientious objector or other level of civil disobedient, a narcotics user from the middle classes with substantial educational background, a black or other minority group militant —all of whom do not have the traditional negative self-image historically associated with criminals. For this group, the term *political prisoner* might be more appropriate. From the frequent interaction between these activists and more traditional inmates at county jails, resulting from the now commonplace *busts,* which are outgrowths of various demonstrations, to the influence of such personages as Phillip and Daniel Berrigan (1971). The modelling and internalization of a strengthened self-concept are closely coupled with the concept that race and class oppression, plus the inequities in the socio economic system make each inmate a *political prisoner* from at least one standpoint. It is these inmates too, who are generally more successful at challenging a given institution's proscribed reading list than were an older breed.

Thirdly, the spirit of social protest now existing in the free community is perhaps the strongest influence. Rebellion in prisons are much more commonly occurring across racial lines, in a similar way to events staged by activists on the outside. Note some of the similarities in the stance between the participants in the lunch-counter sit-ins in the fifties, the continuing passive, if more confrontive, activities of the sixties, including the 1968 Democratic Convention and, more recently, such activities as the 1971 *May Day* demonstrations in Washington, D.C. Each of these actions had in common with the 1971 riot at Attica and other subsequent events, an implicit understanding that the participants vigorously chose to make their point.

These factors are mentioned to alert the correctional counselor to the need to develop a philosophy of rehabilitation in prison, which would incorporate some provision for meeting the influence of these factors, their effects and their impact. These newly needed aspects would be incorporated within whatever model of intervention the counselor utilized. Perhaps a fair analogy can be made with medicine, in which the physician needs to be alerted to new maladies and remedies.

Yet, the careful and insightful counselor must be aware that these changes have done basically nothing but exacerbate the inmate's usual problem of externalizing responsibility, i.e., for failing to accept the consequences of his own behavior. This is another facet of the *Officer-Krupke* syndrome, (Bernstein Record). It translates readily from *I am sick*, to one of *I am sick because you, the community, are sick*. In either option, the onus for change is placed somewhere else *on your shoulders, not mine*.

EXTERNALIZATION OF RESPONSIBILITY

One of the changes brought about by imprisonment is the inmate subculture. Research indicates that the convict code is more generally accepted at a superficial level rather than a level which would cause the internalization of its values by the great majority of the inmate body. Still, the typical inmate derives some benefit, for instance, the restoration of a modicum of dignity to the members. Secondly, the sub culture helps to alleviate the feelings of total subjugation to the captor group's control. Thirdly, it has its own status selection processes, giving for most of its members some viable role, be it merchant, con-leader, etc. This legitimation stands in sharp contrast to that granted the inmate in those roles assigned by the prison staff. The inmate social system then, in some measure, causes the individual inmate to externalize both the responsibility for his behavior and for assuming the initiative for its change.

(The counselor aids in the attempt to ease the inmate into an adjustment to the prison experience.) This creates another obstacle to extra institutional living. The mutually exclusive and contradictory demands in these two living conditions are too well-known to require reiteration. Yet it must be stressed that the institutional-adjustment model has been confused with treatment to the detriment of behavior change which could accrue in this setting, were its effects better understood by correctional workers.

A central quality of most correctional institutions is the authoritarian quality of the structure. This authoritarian setting has strong paranoid elements as one of its components. The sense that one may be *offed* exists within the captor and captive groups as well as between the two groups. It is further seen in the guarded relationship that the correctional institution has to its surrounding community.

Part of the genesis of this problem dates back to times when guards were paid so poorly, that *packing* for inmates and inmate blackmail of the generally less skillful guard-class was normative behavior in prisons. Prior to civil service laws, a more flagrant form of what is called *backstabbing* was a common method of eliminating the competition for higher echelon staff positions within a prison.

CURRENT COUNSELOR ROLES

Perhaps the principle problem in the correctional counselor's role is a seemingly curious phenomenon in which the institution becomes the client rather than the inmate. (In certain counselor-client relationships, the client lacks a share in decision-making that permits him to: 1. choose his counselor; 2. share in the prerogative of setting the basic parameters of the relationship, such as duration, extent, and hours of meetings; and more importantly, to determine the extent of self-divulgency in the relationship.)

There are some unique aspects to counseling in the correctional setting. The effects on both counselor and client — keepers and the kept — are so important to a total understanding of the challenges involved that some discussion of pertinent points seems essential.

The counselor takes part in the inmate's initial adaptation procedure by assisting in aspects of his formal and informal orientation to the institution. Taking data upon intake, the counselor is asked to assess the inmate's attitude toward the offense, ostensibly to aid in making decisions of initial classification, and later at annual reviews, parole hearings, etc. At this point, the counselor is asking the inmate, in effect, to *program him!* Obviously, the inmate knows by the time he reaches the correctional setting that telling how he really feels, or what he thinks of what he did, will probably have an adverse effect upon his chance for an early return to freedom, unless it coincides with the expectations of the counselor and others on the institutional staff. As a result, he *programs* what he thinks the counselor and others want to hear.

The counselor is a prime functionary in the parole process in most institutions today. Parole is bestowed for the most part on those whose institutional behavior has conformed to the *hoop jumping* syndrome of expectations that the treatment and parole staff seem wedded to, rather than any appraisal of how the inmate may be able to function in free society where the real test is. For the inmate population, conformity, measured by its normal criterion, (*programming*), seems to be an invalid way to assess the inmate's ability to live by free-society values. This assumption is partially substantiated by the present high rates of recidivism. As his participation in this *hoop jumping*, the counselor delineates the initial program for the inmate, and establishes the parameters in each phase. The counselor's presentation to the Initial Screening Committee delineates the inmate's structure. This is variously labelled, either a *prescription* or a *program*. It will invariably include bits of education, a little vocational training, portions of group counseling, which is, if available, an interaction of severely limited trust.

ROLES AND VALUES

As an introduction to this portion of the chapter, a presentation of alternate strategies will serve as a useful prelude.

It is easy to understand that one of the prime values of the correctional counselor is that of making an income. His behavior with respect to persons in subordinate positions will be reflected in this value-seeking, as well as his relation and behavior toward superordinates, such as program administrators, deputy wardens, and other higher echelon treatment personnel.

The correctional officer or guard of course, has similar values, as do each of those in the other groups. One of the correctional officers method of defining himself as a *winner* is in seeking to contrast himself with the inmate — to distanciate himself from the inmate — and thereby avoid the contamination of identification with the inmate, with whom he might have many similarities.

The administration in the correctional setting is interested in the same job protection and the chief threat to their emploment security lies in the community and its response to their programs. Behaviorally, this results in the maintenance of an isolated stance from the community because as the news media knows, a *low-profile* is the hardest one for potential critics from the community to shoot at. Unfortunately, this defensive posture on the part of the majority of correctional administrators has greatly interfered with their ability to obtain community support for community-based programs, such as work-release, halfway houses, etc.

Having a clear understanding of what values are being sought will permit the change agent-counselor to select his strategies more effectively. The one value, which each *actor* seeks, is the maintenance of his present employment, i.e., his financial security. If the correctional counselor keeps abreast of current court decisions, which strengthen the civil rights of the inmates, understands which newspaper editors are interested in scrutinizing his institution for political or publicity purposes, then he is in the best position to create change, using each of the aforementioned characteristics of the situation and the *actors* as leverage. For example, an anonymous tip to a newspaper editor, regarding inhumane conditions in some specific aspect of prison life, such as the adjustment area or isolation unit, which represents cruel or inhumane punishment, coupled with an indication of the recent State Supreme Court decisions regarding this violation will cause rapid changes. These will be far more rapid, using this strategy, than sending a memo to the administrator about the effects such conditions have on the mental health of the counselor's client-group. The change agent will then assist the administration by helping them anticipate what their next most visible problem area will be and, using his understanding of human groups and human needs, will begin to show them how to effect changes which would anticipate the possibility of further critical outside scrutiny. Perhaps the astute administrator will begin to realize that, to insure his job security, changes of a qualitative nature will be required.

To indicate that the above discussion is not only ideal, but feasible, I can point to Walla Walla, Washington, where an inmate counsel, elected by the inmates, no longer makes minor recommendations regarding only the expenditure of the recreation budget and what radio programs will be beamed into the cells through the inmates head sets; rather, this unique penitentiary is moving towards total inmate self-government. It is interesting to note that a letter to the editor in a popular journal, in the wake of the 1971 Attica Prison riot, written by the president and secretary of the Walla Walla inmate body, indicates why such a disorder is no longer needed there as a means of seeking a redress of grievances.

ACADEMIC PREPARATION

Planning intervention strategies, tactics, and maneuvers, depends in large part upon the conceptual tools given the counselor in preservice training. Having a theory of rehabilitation, of institutional life, of dehumanization and its effects generally, of authoritarianism and authoritarians, should be a central portion of that training. The training of correctional workers at a professional level has been, in the main, distressing and inadequate. Most professional correctional workers, including persons at the counselor level, do not require more than a BA degree in the social sciences, or an MA and for special positions, at best, an MSW. The masters degree level correctional administration major, at best, will usually have a corrections emphasis within sociology, or other behavioral science. He will read standard texts on criminal typology, sociological analysis of prisons, and the most up-to-date means for rehabilitating the inmate, following the *medical-model*. This, as noted above, is a model dependent upon individual adaptation to the existing social order, essentially a psychogenic orientation to deviance. While problems in corrections are often seen in these writings, far less often are solutions promulgated which could be responsive to the problems which follow assumptions other than those based upon individual adaptation. Especially scarce are indications of the various moral dilemmas, which *prisonization* presents to inmates, to the staff, and the larger community.

The correctional worker, who would be a change agent in the fullest sense, will need to bring back to the academic settings where correctional programs are held, some evidence from the real situation of what these moral dilemmas are in concrete terms. In this way, students and their teachers, who are often many years removed from contact with the institutions, may begin to understand these dilemmas and to learn to seek their resolution in an atmosphere of maximum support for the student. He will not receive such support when conceiving of social change once he has begun work in a correctional establishment.

One of the major hurdles with correctional programs is their lag in knowledge; that is, they are years behind current knowledge of human behavior. A partial solution is to enhance the communication from the academic world to the correctional setting. Those at all levels in the correctional setting: custody, treatment staff and inmates, should all be informed of what current studies show, relative to more efficient models of rehabilitation. This, of course, would necessitate the breaking down of the long-held negative sanction preventing *fraternization* between inmates and staff.

This might involve beginning a journal club in the institution, looking for specific studies, geared to indivdual staff members, which will give them an increased sense of competence and serve their own value system, while enhancing their effectiveness. Additionally, the corrections change agent can feed back information to the school from which he has come, to professors and others, regarding what he is encountering in his work role. He should discuss how they may better prepare oncoming students to deal with some of the problems he has encountered.

A more powerful method of bringing models of rehabilitation from isolated pilot programs to the attention of the entire institution does perhaps exist. A few joint appointments to both a correctional facility and the nearest universities' department of sociology, psychology, corrections, etc., could have a powerful effect, given that viable roles were created for such persons in the institution. More important than their ascribed status, however, would be their strategy as change agents.

IMPEDIMENTS TO CHANGE

The writer has seen programs of some institutions geared to the level of the most unruly, intractable inmate subgroup, and other prisons' programs were geared to the great majority of the inmate body. It can be established from the data that there are less killings, knifings, and a lower level generally of dehumanization in those institutions which followed the latter model.

By the same token, in many institutions, the administration is not sufferng from cognitive dissonance or *folie a deux.* Yet, these administrators while knowing what changes need to be made to better effect the rehabilitation of inmates, fail to make these changes — one likely interpretation is that they fear reprisals from the prison's *old guard.*

The change agent, by establishing himself as a person who knows the most *current theory,* will become part of education and in-service training committees, altering the institution's philosophy. The old guard thereby, either becomes isolated, or *comes around.* I have seen one such instance in a prison. The strategy of the change agent was that people prefer to maximize the meaning their work hold for them, to be as effective as possible in meeting the goal of rehabilitation of the inmate.

A staff in-service training program was elaborated with the ostensible purpose of preparing staff to hold counseling groups. A well-known and respected psychologist, then holding weekly therapy groups for alcoholic imates was asked to do this training. He quickly perceived the need those in attendance were expressing. A need to understand themselves, and their motivation better. By giving heavy positive reinforcement for statements of self-divulgence, the thirty-five or so persons present, from various segments of the institutional staff, a climate of introspection was created. Within a few meetings, persons coming to the *class* were beginning to report on relationships with inmates in which they could relate to the inmate in personal ways to bring about change in the inmates' attitudes, etc. Formerly, the eminance of the prohibition against *fraternization with inmates* would have prevented these relationships.

Unfortunately, the funds supporting the *classes* were cut off, and the program stopped before it had done more than point out the potential multiple consequences of its occurrence.

Persons attending the class openly discussed their own fears, concerns and hopes in a climate of inquiry and positive payoff, whereas normative behavior in institutions for staff, as well as inmates has long been that the staff *do your own time.* Thus, an educational program to train staff to hold counseling groups, in which the teacher modeled and solicited openness and self-indulgence did bring about change in institutional values toward working with inmates.

CHANGE AGENTRY

It is in the area of responsibility for social action that the counselor in a correctional setting needs to be particularly astute in making his definition of the situation, of his personal attributes and deficits, and finally, in planning and pursuing strategies to create desirable change. A personal reflection may serve to illustrate this point.

A few years ago, the writer worked as a correctional counselor at a state prison in a state considered to have one of the most progressive penal systems in the country. During the Christmas seasons of the prior three years, the normally tense racial situation between blacks and whites boiled to near riot conditions. Only one staff person, a black corrections officer, had been able to communicate with and gain the cooperation of a number of black inmates. He had been summoned from his home over forty miles distance to intervene with a group who had *sat down.* This guard, also the staff sponsor of the all black, African Culture Group invited the writer to attend a meeting of the group.

I attended two meetings, addressed the group during the second, and found I could relate to many of their concerns. I then sought to become a facilitator, both for the group as well as between the white and black groups in the prison. The black staff then consisted of three guards and one counselor, none of whom, other than the guard sponsoring the culture group, were interested in getting involved. Subsequently, I asked the deputy warden of treatment if anyone from the staff who was white was able to communicate with this group of more militant black inmates. He indicated that no such person existed, as the policy of the prison was to treat each inmate as an individual and not as a group.

As I felt alien and impotent in the environment, more toward staff than toward inmates, I did not press the matter further. The futility of that prison administration's policy of refusing to acknowledge the presence of problems was later demonstrated forcefully in the *Soledad Brothers* incidents and a number of less sensational matters.

First, I had played ping pong with an inmate in my cell block, during which time three guards, one at a time, passed in front of the cell block's first tier door, staring at this interaction. My simplistic attempt to reduce social distance with inmates resulted in nearly a total ostracism by guards. Later on, I exchanged divergent views on the Vietnam situation with the prison's psychiatrist, who wore a green beret at work. Prior to this discussion, I was to take the leadership of his therapy group, a significant honor. After the exchange, when he decided against this course, I realized my collateral was exhausted.

In the correctional setting, there is particular difficulty in carrying out the prescribed duties of the counselor role when so much occurs of a destructive nature, to both keepers and kept. These dilemmas, in any other setting, would bring the moral individual to an imperative choice-point and force a confrontation.

For this reason, and others which will be elaborated upon below, the writer has always considered correctional work to be a *burn-out* role. One constantly works to change staff attitudes, as well as those of his ostensible clients, or he must emotionally divorce himself from the moral implications of the situation. The latter choice seems to be more popular a solution. This is usually manifested in an alteration of self-concept. The manifestation of this shift is either a cynical attitude toward the role, the clients, and finally toward the self. An authoritarian paternalism is an alternate result which serves a similar end: that of avoiding intimacy and self-disclosure with the client group.

Concerning the possibilities of effecting behavioral change in those inmates where incarceration is a necessity: the counselor must have a theory upon which to base strategies for altering the play of forces in that setting which takes into account what each person in that setting needs in order to define himself as a *winner*. The theoretical basis, which should guide the structuring of the environment for persons for whom the secure care and custody of prison is the only viable resource, is as follows: behavioral change can best be effected by practicing the desired behavior in an environment likely to produce reinforcement in measure and quality which is most similar to the environment in which those behaviors occur naturally. In the absence of a natural environment, in this case the home community of the inmate, simulations of as many aspects of that community, as it relates to the inmate, are needed.

Some of the goals, which a counselor must espouse for inmates in a correctional setting, are those which will specifically effect satisfactory adjustment to free society. This statement implies a logical set of strategies for correctional workers, in general, and for the counselor as the initiator of the institutional program change, in particular. For example, men who are incarcerated for failure to provide child support payments, require treatment strategies and goals which will help them view this obligation as a primary value. (They probably need employment as well.) It has implications, as well, for those men serving time for pedophiliac offenses and for every other type of offender and offense.

To effect program changes within the institution, the initial strategy for the correctional counselor involves gathering a constituency. This is a relatively easy task, as in the early stages of employment he is involved in a *sniffing* game, with other treatment staff members. The change agent makes limited indication of his own philosophical position, with respect to rehabilitation, in a variety of behaviors with both staff and inmates, gaining a reputation as having pro-rehabilitation, as contrasted to a punitive-orientation. If he has some theory and is able to make a viable definition of the situation, he will soon be able to take specific

steps to solidify his position, to gain a constituency, and to enhance his power in the setting, He will then move in those directions where least resistance to change is offered.

The specific changes may fall in the area of making recommendations about handling racial tensions in the institution, about
increase in inmate prerogative towards self-governance, about increases in treatment and custody staff inter-action, through sports
or activities of a recreational nature with other staff. There are
a variety of other small changes, which quickly show staff and
inmates at all levels that he is interested in moving ahead but
that he is not trying to threaten the values that they seek in this
situation, as delineated above.

Perhaps the greatest good that the correctional counselor can
achieve is within the community rather than in the prison. He
has a specific responsibility to make the citizenry, in general, and
policy-makers and opinion-leaders, specifically, aware of those
aspects of our society that are contributing psychic damage and
emotional maladjustment to its members.

The prisons have been loathe to bring on public scrutiny, as
they have been failing with between thirty and ninety-nine percent of their product since before Freud. Further, as much of the
ritual dehumanization, which obtains in the name of maintaining
order, might not stand in a more visible situation. Finally, the
lack of trust, mentioned previously, is another big factor which
is present in correctional administrators when faced with confronting the community with the problems of the prison.

Conversely, the public, generally, does not want to be told of
its complexity in social problems and so, logically, avoids the painful consequence of knowing: involvement in turn produces guilt.
The captive group's lack of ability to become visible, to gain redress of grievances, except in certain cases of capital proportion,
and their reduction by the above-mentioned procedures, to a
state of almost a childlike dependency, lead to the conclusion that
significant change will require multifaceted strategies to effect
and will be quite demanding of the resources of the change agent.

Yet, it is within the larger community, as soon as he has established a firm enough base, that the correctional counselor must
begin to involve himself. Invariably, there are a variety of com-

munity groups who are seeking to have speakers from exotic and strange places. In such engagements, the change agent will begin to make contact with those individuals in the community, who are able to see some fundamental problems, i.e. society as unwilling to accept the ex-felon as a member and where the inmate has been scapegoated for the society's benefit. This phenomenon is well-stated in the words of G.H. Mead (1918), "Hostility towards the law-breaker unifies all members of the community in the emotional solidarity of aggression against the offender." The correctional counselor then begins to pass the ball to interested and influential community members, toward enhancing qualitative change with respect to programs both within and outside the institutional setting.

CONCLUSIONS

One basic fallacy of incarceration as a vehicle for securing behavior change, rests on the assumption that removal from the community is a viable way of teaching the inmates to learn new behaviors, which will again generalize and transfer to the community. Even if it were more optimally efficient, this is a very poor substitute for holding some measure of external control on an offender and assisting him in a variety of ways, with changing behavior, while still within the free community. The thesis advanced in this chapter is that the great majority of inmates do not require secure care and custody because they do not present a threat of physical harm to self and others. They can be monitored in open society.

Those who are a chronic threat will be the only offenders requiring incarceration in a setting as removed from conditions of the free world as are found in a prison. For many people, having acute behavior control problems, temporary removal to a county jail or other secure setting closer to the individual's community is a preferable solution, as the offender will still be able to maintain contact with those persons from his usual environment. The positive aspects of this environment and what may be supplemented, the therapeutic resources from the community of which he is a member, all are immediately available as assets in aiding the offender in making changes.

The wise correctional counselor must know how to divide his activities so that he does not spend more viability than he can build up, until he is ready to leave the setting. There are two chief considerations: (1) the degree of change sought on the one hand, which almost always has a one to one relationship with the amount of personal censure, which the interventionist will incur; (2) the amount of personal resources or ego strength which he has available.

The writer has the belief, based upon more than ten years in the field, that the correctional interventionist needs to have a safe haven, found in some contrasting work, or *R and R* in effect. This is because the encrusted, isolated condition of the correctional setting finally leads the most well-equipped change agent towards unconscious conformity and a blunting of insights regarding situations which were, at first, quite obvious. One method of minimizing this blunting is by maintaining touch stones outside the setting of both a personal and professional nature. These must be maintained to keep an external frame of reference from being lost.

In summary, prison should be used as a last resort. Each succeeding step of increasing loss of prerogative of decision-making regarding the offender's own life should be considered prior to prison. This conclusion is based on the principle that the level of independent functions that a convicted offender can sustain must be retained, insofar as possible. After it is lost through adjustment to prison routine, it is difficult and unlikely to be re-learned completely.

The counselor, in making his definition of the situation, will be aware of each individual and will structure each situation in accord with this dictum. With inmates, the change agent must be acutely aware of what considerations cause men to accept responsibility for their behavior and promote such conditions within the prison. He must be able to help inmates recognize peer leaders who are able to effect behavior change in themselves and others in accord with a functional model.

Finally, he needs to use his professional skill to facilitate understanding and communication between groups: those with a vested interest in maintaining the existing situations and those of academic and other persuasions with alternate views.]{He must do this to alleviate human distress within the community, to effect constructive social change, and to better effect attitudinal and behavioral change of deviant-group members.] In this, he has both an obligation as a professional with a special body of knowledge and as a citizen toward exerting whatever pressure he can in the body politic to further such change.

REFERENCES

1. Bernstein, L. (music) and Sondheim, L. (lyrics): *West Side Story*. Columbia Masterworks Records, OL5238.
2. Berrigan, D. and Coles, R.: *The Georgraphy of Faith*. Beacon Press, Boston, 1971, pp.1-33.
3. Goffman, I.: *Asylums*. Anchor Books, Garden City, 1961, pp. 18-66.
4. Mead, G.: The Psychology of punitive justice. *American Journal of Sociology, 23*:585-592, 1918.
5. Mitford, Jessica: Kind and usual punishment in California. *The Atlantic, 3*:52, 1970.
6. Schrag, P. The Ellsburg affair. *Saturday Review, 14*:37, 1971.

CHAPTER VII

REALITY AND DILEMMA OF WOMEN'S PRISONS

Sharon J. Copeland

"To live outside the law you must be honest"
Bob Dylan

T HE AIM OF this chapter is to focus on some problems of the women's penitentiaries and to offer some tentative suggestions for improvement.

Historical Influences

Block and Geis (1962) note that:

From the code of Hammurabi, up to the contemporary judicial system, reference is made to the religious biblical heritage of our society. The code is the first legal document that reflects explicit provisions to cultivation and maintenance of the land. It mirrors the rigid social stratification of the freeman, the serfs, and the slaves. It reflects the religious tone of our society.

It was not until the early 1900's that women became involved in correctional reform. Their foot slid in the door under the auspices of religion. Grunhut (1948) had described some of the women who had the most influence on the prison system, noting that, "In 1813, however, Mrs. Elizabeth Fry was introduced to visit Newgate (a prison in England) by the representative of its state, made by some persons of the Society of Friends (a social movement organization) to which she belonged." Mrs. Fry talked with the women prisoners and observed that the women had two

74

main needs: (1) ". . . to be treated as human beings, (2) that their multitudes of children confined with them should be occupied and educated." She made no decisions without the cooperation of the women. She organized a welfare work committee in 1817, called the Ladies' Association for the Improvement of the Female Prisoners in Newgate. She initiated work programs, visiting programs, and monitors and matrons to keep the prison orderly and bring dignity back to the lives of the prisoners. One principal objective Mrs. Fry had in mind was to have the government pay for and take over the provision of employment for women prisoners. Mrs. Fry maintained that women should be looked after by women, classified according to their character and degree of criminality; that there should be adequate necessities of dress, warmth, food, and bedding, along with a work-release program after parole. Mrs. Fry's views, balanced with insight and practical humanity for incarcerated, were far advanced beyond her time. Mrs. Sarah Martin followed in her footsteps by, "providing for many of the needs of women prisoners: moral welfare, employment while serving their sentences, and aid on their eventual discharge from prison."

Alice Tyler (1944) writes, "In America, the Philadelphia Society for Alleviating the Miseries of Public Persons was the first —and for a long time the most effective—of such organizations, and its work was copied by philanthropists in other communities."

The most renowned women reformer who influenced corrections in America was Dorthea Dix. Alice Tyler (1944) writes,

In 1841 Dorthea Dix was asked to take a Sunday School class in the women's department of the House of Corrections in East Cambridge. Shocked at the deplorable conditions of the prisoners, her sympathy was aroused and led her to search for aid to make public aware of the prison conditions. Beginning with the famous pledge, "I tell what I have seen," she proceded to call attention to the present state of insane persons confined with the commonwealth in cages, closets, cellars, stalls—pens—chained, naked, beaten with rods and lashed into obedience!

With dedication and much social criticism, these women helped reform the criminal institutions to a gentler doctrine of regeneration.

Men's versus Women's Incarceration

Women's needs and roles in life are different from men's needs and roles in prison. During the 1900's, even the most enlightened writers and statesmen of the time considered the needs of women prisoners to be different from those of men prisoners. The fact that much criminality among women does not reach the courts, perhaps reflects this phenomenon. To quote Betty Freidan (1963), "Women, ideally emancipated in our society, continue to receive financial support even when a marriage is dissolved, do not compete on an equal basis with men in the job market, and continue to be principally concerned with being 'homemakers'." This is particularly true for women in prison, as the majority are not usually trained for careers. Homemaking is their prominent life style on the outside of prison. Society is able to deal with anti social conduct of women by means much more stringent than those imposed on men. Women prisoners have often been a forgotten minority, separated from their male fellow prisoners. Women prisoners are expected to carry the ordinary prison routine with a minimum of regard for their special needs.

Women's Imprisonment

The prison's physical plant depends on money. Each state varies in its accommodations. Galvin (1969) refers to the trend of separate institutions when he notes that, "Many states, however, have provided separate institutions for their female offenders, and today there are thirty-one institutions which house female offenders only." The institution may be cottage style or one large facility which houses all the requirements, surrounded by fencing, and topped with barbed wire. The center of the institution is usually arranged around a central lawn with geraniums and pansies, (no one has ever explained why these flowers are most often chosen) where the women visit during the summer months.

The process of incarceration generally goes something like this: Upon arrival, the convict sees the supervisor or correctional counselor, who gathers data to be entered on the warden's list. The convict is then assigned to her cell, which has been previously decided upon by the personnel, supposedly to enhance

the resident's so called *personal development*. By the end of
the month, if the prison has the money and staff, psychological
testing is done, educational grade level is determined; and maybe
one, (or two, at the most) chats with the correctional counselor
has taken place. The status of the prisoner depends largely upon
her classification. Ward and Kassebaum (1965) write:

> Former identities become meaningless, and new labels become rele-
> vant. A woman who has been officially designated as a "criminal"
> can also be more specifically labeled as a murderer, drug addict,
> arsonist, forger, and so forth, thus increasing the identification with a
> criminal lifestyle.

The freedom and movement of the women is centered around
a rigid schedule, demanding participation from each of the residents. Adjustment to the routine of prison life is determined by
the personnel staff, who consider the following factors in making
their judgment. Among the adjustment *items* are, getting up on
time and attending meals, duty assignments, talking politely with
the staff members, and maybe attending Sunday church services.
To the women, it usually means learning the institutional routine, *psyching out* all the staff members' idiosyncracies, and
squelching the internal sizzling hate, boredom and despair, by
lying and playing *games* with the staff, as well as with each
other. The inmates' informal code provides as much control and
predictability as the formal prison system norms. Ward and
Kassebaum (1965) mention that, "the inmates' social system is
generalized in part because of the need for stable patterns of
expectations and frames of reference." Instead of growing in
trust, each inmate is on guard. After a period of prescribed
good behavior, the inmate is allowed to participate in academic
or vocational training which may lead to a G.E.D. or certificate
in such fields as nursing, hair styling, cosmetology, and assignments to work duties of cooking, painting, housekeeping, laundry,
sewing, yard work, etc.

Mail is censored and often restricted to a few pages. Inmates
may receive daily mail, if the writer is on the approved check list.

Visiting for the residents is again determined by the staff. Each
visitor must be placed on the approved visiting list. Each resident

may be visited by her spouse once a week. The residents' children and friends may visit them twice a month. Depending on architectural design and money, visits may take place in an open visiting room, where many visits occur simultaneously. These visits are observed by a staff member to model and prescribe appropriate behavior. Yet the prime motive is to deter the passing of contraband. The atmosphere of the visiting room is generally pleasant—it does not have all the barbed wire cubicles that people imagine. Still, it is restrictive in an emotional sense. Visitors and inmates do not express their full feelings. Later in the evening, in the quiet of the cells, tears are often shed.

Into the tightly scheduled day and its interims of limited freedom and movement, the count takes place. This usually happens three times a day in the assigned locations to account for each resident's presence. If anything is suspected by the staff, searches may take place at this point, in the inmates' rooms or on their person. As Goffman (1961) accurately notes, for the hardened experienced con, "violation of the code prohibiting ratting has resulted in the imposition of the most severe punitive sanctions inmates can apply, including death."

Emotional Effects of Imprisonment

It is the rare judge who sentences a woman to prison for her first offense. Hence, there is an accepted bias of confining lower class and minority group persons. Women incarcerated in prison usually have a long delinquent and criminal record.

There are several pains associated with imprisonment. Perhaps the most painful is separation from loved ones. Another pain is loss of autonomy and liberty. Imprisonment is a regimented lifestyle and is felt keenly by the inmates, who, by and large, enjoy prescribed freedom of movement and self-expression. Denial of inmate ownership of personal goods and choice of dress code and hair style is deeply resented by most women. The inmate is hard pressed not to view the prison system as a direct attack on her self-image. The lack of heterosexual relationship is frustrating for most inmates, and the forced proximity to other women results in homosexual activity for some; and repulsion, insecurity, and hate for others. The constant gossip engenders ostracism, lack of trust, and *snitching*.

Coping Methods for Pains of Imprisonment

In an attempt to cope with life in a prison, some women withdraw, both physically and psychologically. This withdrawal allows them to *escape* within the prison by creating *a life within a life* style. Although an exterior appearance of conformance to prison life style is rigidly maintained (protected) internally, the women create a wide variety of *satisfying* lies and become experts in their autistic life styles.

Another method of dealing with her isolation and aloneness might result in homosexual relationships. Ward and Kassebaum (1965) make note that:

> While some data on the incidence of female homosexuality in the larger community has been collected by Kinsey and his associates, the general neglect of the women's prison as an object of study is reflected in the fact that there is virtually no reliable information available on the incidence of homosexuality among adult female prison inmates. Surprisingly, Glueck's exhaustive study of *500 Delinquent Women* does not mention homosexuality in their study of the characteristics and behavior of adult female prisoners.

Among women who are isolated from men, feelings and display of affection normal to the outside world leads readily to erotic contact. Once again, to quote from Ward and Kassebaum (1965):

> The behavior of both butches and femmes is likely to get them into disciplinary trouble, but in some cases the willingness to take strong action, such as rebuking a staff member to her face and the serving of time in the primitive segregation unit, is viewed as a test of the degree of love and loyalty for one's partner.

Other inmates become involved in homosexual relations because they have less experience with men, or their experience with men has been unhappy. Some women become involved because they are unattractive and have few, if any, skills to attract a loving relationship with men. Fear of bearing children, fear of loneliness, efforts to punish family members, lovers, or other significant persons on the outside for having failed to prevent incarceration, tend to be other reasons for acting out sexually while women are in prison.

Ward and Kassebaum (1965) make an accurate observation:

> We do not know whether sexual deprivation is more keenly or more easily recognized as time increases, but it can be said that during the first weeks in prison, sexual frustration is only one of the many new frustrations, and it is during this time that most of the women turn out. It is our contention then, that physical deprivation of heterosexual outlets or the attractiveness of another woman as a sexual object is less important in motivating homosexuality than are the social and psychological benefits that accrue to such ties.

What is known is that most of the women return to heterosexual involvement when they leave the prison. For these women, it seems that homosexual activity was situational, whereas, for women who entered the prison espousing homosexuality, the problem is indigenous, and not situational.

Treatment Staff and the Relation to Inmates

The availability of help for the inmates, in their efforts to deal with their problems is minimal, Merton (1959) observes:

> Events aimed at expanding treatment functions result in shifting compromise on the treatment level; whereas custody, internal control, and economic self-sufficiency emerge as relatively more important in the prison's hierarchy of goal status.

Galvin's (1969) study of the thirty-one institutions for women in the states suggests:

> these institutions tend to be quite small, averaging 191 inmates per institution in 1967. One had only eight inmates. Eight institutions had more than three hundred prisoners. The largest house 897. In the case of treatment and training staff, the ratio was 31.1 to 1, as contrasted with the overall figure of 31.3 to 1. Eleven institutions had less than 1.5 inmates per treatment and training staff member, and less than twenty inmates per treatment and training staff member. Only six institutions had more than three inmates per staff member and more than thirty inmates per rehabilitation specialist.

The prison divides the duties of personnel into specialized assignments. The treatment staff typically consists of: caseworker supervisor, correctional counselor, and other personnel who help the inmates, teachers, medical personnel, and work supervisors. If the prison has the money, specialists trained in therapy and group work are available; there is a growing trend in this direction.

The assigned casework supervisor prepares individual social histories for the purposes of institutional classification and assignment. This is relative to the resident's security classification—classified as maximal or minimal. Other duties of the casework supervisor are setting up treatment goals, obtaining and reviewing court and family information, and consulting with others in the institution regarding evaluation. The casework supervisor follows up to see that the treatment plan is implemented.

The correctional counselors, who *live with* the residents during eight hour shifts, have the responsibility of writing reports on inmate adjustments activities, and behavior. Since priorities are set, the correctional counselors are usually, *bogged down* having to spend forty per cent of their time in administrative paper work, reading mail, or attending staff meetings. The resident may be seen periodically for personal problems. The usual stance, however, is to leave the resident to work out her problem with other residents. or through letters, visitors, or just plain alone, rather than with the counselor. The reports written by the correctional counselor are placed in each inmate's file (or jacket). These are most important since reviewing boards take these reports into consideration for parole. Sentencing and parole differ in varying states, but the indeterminate sentence is the most known and also the most controversial. Block and Geis (1962) state:

> . . . the indeterminate sentencing laws of the state preclude not only the possibility of knowing when one can be paroled, but prior to the initial board appearance, an inmate does not know at what date parole eligibility will be considered.

Yet many prisoners prefer it, saying it gives them hope and that their prison behavior is *worth something*, while other prisoners feel they are at the mercy of the prison staff.

Another important type of therapist is the group therapist, or group leader. The group therapist may be the institutional psychologist, a correctional counselor, social worker, teacher, nurse, or office clerk. Most group leaders have received some in-service training. The effect of group therapy programs depends on meaningful communication between staff and residents. Often times in women's prisons the staff does not have the skill to break through the informal codes, or the staff may not have the knowledge or time to help the residents work out solutions to existing problems. Lack of funding for a therapeutic trained staff is a major deterrent. The reader can refer to Chapter VIII, in which a thorough discussion of methods and techniques is presented for group therapy for male prisoners.

Feminine Trends in Society

As stated earlier, women sentenced to prison usually have a long delinquent past criminal record. It is an unusual judge who sentences a woman to prison for her first offense. Ester Harding (1970) in her book, *The Way of All Women*, reflects:

> It almost seems that America is moving toward a matriarchal state of society, in which a strong efficient woman marries a rather underdeveloped and feminine man who takes a filial relation to her. The woman is everything — mother, provider, organizer — and the man merely an adjunct, however, necessary to the household.

Assuming, therefore, that women are becoming more masculine, it would be my opinion that: (1) They will be involved in more crime-related acts of a more masculine nature in the future. (2) Since it is rather well known that delinquent girls or ex-convict women can be as aggressive and hostile as any man, this factor should be taken into considerations. Still, today it is usually after a long series of forgery, prostitution, and, infrequently, murder, before a woman is sentenced to prison. Deeper insight into these women's background often reveals an almost abnormal lack of emotions and an indifference to the motives which normally guide the behavior of most women. Albert Cohen (1955), in his book, *Delinquent Boys*, states that, "Female delinquency is relatively specialized, centering around the lack of her self-image as a woman which gives her assurance of her sexual attractiveness." In simple terms, these women hurt. It is the author's view that a profession should specialize in correctional work. Since social workers are concerned with both social problems and human behavior, they seem most appropriate. If so, why are women social workers not committing themselves to work in women's prisons?

The Need for Social Work Specialists in Corrections

There are challenges for the professional working in a women's prison. The professional must avoid either extreme of being frustrated much of the time or accepting the despair and cynicism of the system. Frankly, women social workers have not generally committed themselves to work within corrections, either in the penal institutions or even in the community. The prison system typically resists flexibility and change. Rose Giallombardo (1966) states, "Formal organizations that attempt to minimize both punishment and treatment-oriented goals will be characterized by internal conflict." This largely reflects the rigid prison goals of custody and retribution.

In order to be effective, women social workers need: (1) an extensive knowledge of human behavior, and a background of criminology and its causative factors, (2) preferably, a Masters Degree in Correctional Rehabilitation and Administration. (3) They need a philosophical base which would allow them to understand society and its prevalent social values. (4) They need a knowledge of institutional thinking and an ability to innovate change and an ability to specialize. (5) They need extensive therapeutic skills to fight against the despair, depersonalization, and dependence that the *rubber walls* contribute to the inmates' pain.

Some Problems Social Workers Face in Working with the Inmates

The system's rigid routine results not in maturity, but rather regression. The emotional maturity of the women is stunted upon entrance, and the system furthers this depletion of personality growth. Secondly, due to stature of severe punishment, of stripping one of status and power, the residents mistrust of anyone who makes gestures of help.

Although much of the literature on delinquency and criminality deals with the two categories as one, it is not a good inference that they are the same phenomenon. Certainly a large portion of juvenile delinquents never go on to commit adult crimes, nor do all adult criminals have records of juvenile delinquency. I have seen fit to separate the two in this chapter. Where a study is made, the majority of case histories reveal deprivation of nurture and nature, violence, and lack of education. Additionally, there is a natural correlation between the fact that the majority of women who have a long history of delinquency have never learned to trust. One does not teach trust. Trust comes with experience and someone is always needed to model it. Thirdly, the inmates can sense the social worker's conflicts in working within the system and will try to manipulate her.

The social worker's philosophical base of self-determination is contrary to punishment and incarceration. This principal maintains, as Friedlander (1958) stated, ". . . the individual who is an economic, personal, or social need has the right to determine for himself what his needs are and how they should be met." The significant change in the inmate will occur only when she is helped to help herself. The support of the social worker is an essential factor in her growth for independence.

Fourth, the agencies within the community do not generally work directly with the prison unless an inmate has had previous contact with them before incarceration. The lack of community involvement and resources make the role of the social worker ineffective. The community generally is not amendable to the prison's community. Most communities seemingly deny the realities of prisons.

Women prisoners who have children most frequently come in contact with child welfare agencies. For the most part, contact involves finding foster homes or institutional placement for their children. This may encourage a cyclical webb of criminality. The literature consistantly indicates that broken homes have much more of an impact on girls in contributing to delinquency than it does for delinquent boys.

Lastly, and subjectively, America's socialization process for women does not allow her to endure, for long, the brutality of what human nature is capable. Women in America are generally protected and naive to the cold facts of reality—in sharp contrast, the women prisoners are not. Social work women need to be *tough-minded* and knowledgable about *raw* reality, and not sympathetic and easily conned. Womanhood has been occupied with householding and the responsibilities of upbringing as the major profession, for the most part. Other women, for only short periods of their lives, may be devoted to service-related fields, such as social work, nursing, teaching, etc. Erik Erikson wrote an article called, *Inner and Outer Space: Reflections on Womanhood* (1964), where he depicted how the basic differences in sex roles vary according to style of life and cultural patterns. Erickson ends the article with, "Since a woman is never not a woman, she can see her long-range goals only in those modes of activity which include and integrate her natural disposition." For the woman prisoner, it is critical that she seek to minimize her resentments and maximize her adaptains to womanhood.

Corrections Today

A perusal of the literature shows that interest in correctional reform is cyclical. In the *International Journal of Psychiatry*, Halleck (1968) discusses a historical review of the criminal and the role of psychiatrists in correctional history and rehabilitation. I find it incredible that he did not mention the women's prisons. Today, correctional institutions are in the limelight because crime is increasing. The extensive wave of riots that have recently pervaded the country has lead to an increased examination of prisons. Some ex-convicts are forming groups, such as The National Prisoners' Alliance, to influence the prison system. In America, the character and frequency of crime reflects our conditions of history and our cultural and psychological characteristics of our objectives and aspirations. Block and Geis (1962) accurately write:

> . . . to say, therefore, that crimes reflect the culture and social structure is of little significance unless we recognize the variety of interrelated patterns which may alter the meaning of common values for different groups and different individuals in the society, and which may deflect or impede the attainment of certain goals for different members of the society.

This could be one reason for the inconsistencies in our frontier ethic and persent day cultural characteristics. On the one hand, our past and present is filled with violence and nonconformity, and on the other hand, the ethics of championing the underdog is exposed.

Possible Solutions Within the Prisons

While working in the prison system to bring about change, social workers need to understand that our judicial system is deeply ingrained in tradition, and, as a result, change will be slow. Therefore, the solutions are not to be found in superficial welfare aspects, but in its philosophical depths.

There are many theories of criminality. Sutherland's *Principles of Criminology* seemingly presents the most comprehensive in understanding of criminology. Sutherland and Cressey (1960) present a theory of *differential association*. It is a good starting point. Their paradigm consists of nine integral phases. The basic belief is that crime is fundamentally a form of learning. One is not born a criminal, but learns to become a criminal. After an intellectual framework is grounded (as mentioned above) social workers need to deal with the value structure of the prison system, which subtly stresses dependency—a value structure which fosters a weak and helpless status. The structural norms and rules of the prison are not condusive to risk-taking of a constructive nature. The question could be raised, are the women allowed to decide dress and hair styling according to their own wishes? Without taking risks, how are these women to learn social skills? Positive reinforcement begets growth.

A possible second solution to working within the prison is to be aware of the existential dilemmas of today's world. Social workers need to be alert to experiences of fear, hope, emotional death, subjective time, boredom, courage, etc. Indeed, philosophy! A valuable framework that can be employed is Erik Erickson's (1964) virtue schedule: "I will, therefore, speak of Hope, Will, Purpose and Competence as the rudiments of virtue developed in childhood; of Fidelity as the adolescent virtue: and of Love, Care and Wisdom as the central virtues of adulthood." After social workers have a strong understanding of growth patterns for a person, they need a wide range of treatment skills. Social workers need to be able to state clearly what treatment style they are using—Rogerian, Reality Therapy, Confrontation, or Action techniques, such as Gestalt or Psychodrama, etc. Then social workers need to evaluate which mode of treatment is most effective in working with each type of personality.

Thirdly, social workers need to become advocates for the women prisoners and help bring about change in the prison system. An illustrative example could be to help the system explore and combat the segregation of men from women. Generally, people from healthy backgrounds learned healthy functioning through encouragement and support not from punishment and denial. Association with male prisoners would be a deterrent against homosexual deviance within the prison. Surely other problems could arise, such as sexual acting out, but if the environment is protected and well staffed, the women and men would learn to deal and cope with the problems realistically. In Chapter XI, we note that male and female prisoners on work-release, living in separate *centers*, meet jointly for group therapy. This is a new phase for therapy in corrections.

Fourth, social workers need to help relate institutional life to what happens outside of the prison. For those who have worked in or who have been in prison, there is an awareness of the extreme anxiety and fear that a resident feels the day she is parolled. As her day of departure draws near the woman is tortured with internal questions of survival on the outside. She puzzles in her mind questions of breaking the law again, of getting a job, of how people will treat her, of again making decisions for herself. In order to make this adjustment to the outside world, classes should be conducted on both theory and practicum as one's options. It is my contention that doing and action are the real test of motivation. My suggestions afford a woman prisoner a *head start* toward adjustment, once released. Pre-release classes should be held after parole for follow-up. Those women capable of higher education or specialized training of sorts would be more inclined to follow through on the outside, if they were adequately helped on the inside.

Possible Solutions Within the Community

Efforts, both private and public, should be developed to intensify cooperation between the prison and community. For example, groups should be formed within the community of husbands and relatives who have wives and daughters imprisoned. This would provide support and understanding to the family until the resident returns home.

The trend for providing support is the prerelease center. As Galvin reported (1969), "Only nineteen prerelease centers were reported; six in the federal and one in each of four states. It is known, however, that some were missed, since they were reported in the survey as part of camp systems."

Galvin (1969) further states, that, "Community-based centers were quite small, averaging about twenty-five residents. There were about three inmates per staff member and seven per treatment and training staff member. Typically, the staff consisted of a center director, his assistant, and an employment placement worker." These centers are increasing, but I wonder if it is not a matter of luck whether a prisoner is assisted by the person or organization best able to fit her particular needs.

Social workers within the community should be working closely with the correctional staff on the inmates' problems. Secondly, M.S.W.'s should be allowed to do research in the institutions through investigation, accumulation of data with concise, careful reports. Graduate students in social work could do their thesis on many aspects of prison life as a field placement. Third, M.S.W.'s should work closely with other sciences to gain broader support and understanding from other fields, i.e., psychology, sociology, and anthropology. Fourth, M.S.W.'s should become advocates of women prisoners in the community and in the state level, to help secure financial support for necessary personnel, building, and equipment. Fifth, volunteers, paraprofessionals, and ex-inmates should be encouraged to help the residents in whatever capacity that is needed. For example, they could provide the manpower to take the residents on outings and field trips, to make their adjustment to the outside more predictable and less hazardous. Sixth, M.S.W.'s could help reduce barriers to employment posed by discrimination, the misuse of criminal records and maintenance of rigid job qualifications. If any institution is neglected and misunderstood, it is the prison. Following is a vignette of a woman prisoner:

My name is Wadina. I am an American Indian. I spent sixteen months in prison as a numbered nonentity. I hated it, but discovered later, it helped.

I was born on a reservation in a primitive little grey town. My memories are of drunken cowboys, hollaring and shooting guns, riding horseback, after a drive of long-horned cattle was herded through the center of town. After that, my family was on the move. We went to Butte, Montana, so Dad could work in the mines. It didn't work out so we lived like the story, *Grapes of Wrath*. Five kids, a father with dreams, and a mother who loved to drink camped out across the states, picking fruit and working on ranches. With money depleted, we moved back to the reservation and homesteaded Kom Kan, The Land of the Springs. Things went well for a year, Dad building a log cabin, and Mom feeding the animals, and us kids chasing porcupines and deer. Then Mom began to drink; Father got mad; and us kids began to play *nasties* in the barn. Everytime I turned around, Mother brought home a new baby. Father said they were not his babies, so he took to drinking and gambling.

After that, home became juvenile court, welfare workers, and foster parents. I love the juvenile home because a lady, Mrs. —— made me her pet. Then I got homesick. I wanted Mother and Father, so I ran away. Here I began my institutional days. At five years of age, I was most at home in jail. The authorities would catch me, ship me off to foster homes, and I'd run away again—back to juvenile court, then my family, then foster homes. It never ended. Most of the foster homes had children of their own, so I was never a favorite; I only felt I belonged in a few. I wanted most to be home with my brothers and sisters, Mom and Dad, and Kom Kan, the place I loved.

At ten years of age, I went home again to Mother. She had a new boyfriend and still loved to drink. Wild parties introduced me to necking with old men. I saw intercourse first hand and homosexual affairs. It scared me, until I learned to drink, too. Then it didn't hurt so much. I was on the move, with no time to feel sorry. Besides, Mother had *class*. She beat up an engineer riding a train and drove it down the tracks herself. It took four guys to pull her out.

At fifteen, I received an inheritance—$20,000—and I wanted it. So,

I decided to get married. Within six months time the money was spent. I was on booze and dope heavily, and my husband beat me up frequently. After being shot at, kicked around, and beaten, I divorced him in one year. My elder sister, who was well into crime, put me under her wing, and I began a new life style. Being in dope and booze heavily I didn't care. At eighteen years of age, I was running with *off men*, that is, hired gunmen, prostitutes, dopers—just plain *rip-offs*. Why, in five minutes my sister and I *ripped off* $2,300 in jewelry from ———. We cashed $640 worth of checks in four hours, among other things.

Getting caught was ugly—my sister ate some bad checks and hid false ID cards up her vagina!

The trial was unfair. I was sentenced to two years on the first offense. The reason was because my sister had so many beefs pending, and they wanted to get her on a federal rap. I would not snitch, so I got sent up, too.

County jail was great for thirty-nine days. The trustees were my friends—we sneaked in booze and took turns *balling*.

Prison was terrifying! Walking around the big walls of the men's *joint* to the little *joint* made me shiver. All I could think of was my sister is there. She'll protect me from homosexuals, baby killers, lames and murders.

The stint was not as bad as I thought, except for Mrs. ———, the main supervisor. Everyone hated her, including me. Not having any privacy killed most of my feelings. I did not want anyone to know what I felt or thought. None of the girls stuck together. They would snitch on the least little thing.

The best part of being in prison was the MDTA program. After eight months, I was sent to Beauty School for training. It did me a lot of good, 'cuz I had some purpose to my time. If it would't have been for training and the fact that I was a short-timer, I would have ended up frozen in hate, like many of the women there. In fact, my feelings are just coming back. I could give you more feeling today if I wasn't on a diet and speed pills.

After I got out, I didn't have a thing to my name. I had an apartment rented that some friends were keeping for me. After sitting alone for a week in a blank stare, with few clothes, no pots and pans, and no friends, I called up my counselor from MDTA and told her

I didn't know what to do. She took me by the hand and helped me to do my shopping and begin a new life. I was grateful.

Later, a friend from prison got out and introduced me to some of her friends. I met Joseph, a guy who had been in prison three times, the last for 7½ years on an armed robbery charge. I don't know what he was in for the other two times. We went together for eight months, and I got pregnant. He didn't know, because I didn't tell him. It was a year later, after Stockly was born, that we got back together.

Now we've been married for two years. He is brilliant and is working on his Master's Degree in Criminology, on student loans. He is teaching me a lot. Our baby is our meaning. The only thing that would make me go gack to prison is if I lost Joseph and Stockly. If I go to prison again for any length of time, I'm afraid I would turn *hard-core*. It is easy to hate, and the girls down there teach the ropes good—real good. I learned a lot about life and people; that is, what not to be and do. The first time helped, but the second would kill me.

I worry about my sister. She is worse than ever and will probably be back in prison soon. I hope she doesn't suck me in again, as she brought stolen T.V.'s and rifles to my house the other day. It was hard, but I have to say *NO* to her. There's just me, Joseph, and Stockly now being in the world. My mom is still drunk, and my dad is off someplace, and my other brothers and sisters are scattered around, being *rip-offs*. There's only me, Joseph, and Stockly and being in the world.

As the case example illustrates, the most positive thing about prison life is that it is protecting these women from society. Their inadequacy, lack of education and skill does not allow them to cope or deal with the pressures of society. Even if prisons were cleared overnight of women who should not be there, and only those who should were kept, the success of any prison system would depend upon those who bear the burden of watching over and rehabilitating offenders. By understanding the historical influences, routine of prison life, care and treatment, advocation of some specialization and possible solutions, the prestige of the service will be raised. This is the key to all progress and improvements for women in prisons. As Bob Dylan said in 1964, "Ah, my friends from the prison, they ask unto me, 'How good, how good does it feel to be free?' And I answer them most mysteriously, 'Are birds free from the chains of the skyway?' "

REFERENCES

1. Block, A. and Geis, G.: *Man, Crime, and Society.* Random, New York, 1962.
2. Cohen, A.: *Delinquent Boys, The Culture of the Gang.* The Free Press, New York, 1955.
3. Dylan, B.: *Blond on Blond,* from *Absolutely Sweet Marie.* Columbia Recording, Nashville.
4. Dylan, B.: *Another Side of Bob Dylan,* from *Ballard in Plain D.* Columbia Marcus Reg. Printed in U.S.A., 1964.
5. Erickson, E.: *Insight and Responsibility.* W. W. Norton, New York, 1962.
6. Erickson, E.: Inner and outer space: reflections on womanhood. *Daedalus, 93:*582-606, 1964.
7. Friedan, Betty: *The Feminine Mystique.* Penquin Books Ltd., 1963.
8. Friedlander, W.: *Concepts and Methods of Social Work.* Prentice-Hall, Englewood Cliffs, 1958.
9. Galvin, J. and Karacki, L.: Manpower and training in correctional institutions. Staff Report of Joint Commission on Correctional Manpower and Training. Washington, 1969, p. 24.
10. Giallombardo, Rose: *Society of Women: A study of a Women's Prison.* John Wiley, New York, 1966.
11. Goffman, E.: *Asylums, Essays on the Social Situation of Mental Patients and Other Inmates.* Doubleday & Co., New York, 1961.
12. Goffman, E.: *Stigma Notes on the Management of Spoiled Identity.* Prentice-Hall, Englewood Cliffs, 1965.
13. Grunhut, M.: *Penal Reform.* Oxford Press, New York, 1948.
14. Halleck, S.: American psychiatry and the criminal. *International Journal of Psychiatry. 6:*185-213, 1968.
15. Harding, Ester: *The Way of All Women.* Putnam's and Sons, New York, 1970.
16. Merton, R.: *Sociology of Today.* Basic Books, New York, 1959.
17. Sutherland, E. and Cressey, D.: *Principles of Criminology.* Lippincott, Philadelphia, 1960.
18. Tyler, Alice: *Freedom's Ferment.* University of Minnesota Press, 1944, p. 304.
19. Ward, D. and Kassebaum, G.: *Women's Prison, Sex and Social Structure.* Alding, Chicago, 1965.

CHAPTER VIII

GROUP THERAPY
IN A STATE PRISON

Edward M. Scott

C ONDUCTING GROUP THERAPY in a state prison is a difficult and challenging professional task.]

I will attempt to delineate the fundamentals of this kind of professional task. Hopefully, this will enable the reader to obtain *a feeling* for what happened, as well as a knowledge of concepts and techniques employed. This kind of information should be of assistance to the reader in his own endeavors in similar settings.

As I considered the various methods, techniques, and theories on group therapy (as well as my own twenty years of experience) I felt the following elements to be basic:

1. To be *real* myself—to be a man. Previously, working with male juvenile delinquents, it was rather obvious to me, that the *personal element* has to come before techniques.
2. To be selective and flexible in group therapy methods—not to *sell* any one technique.
3. To utilize educational materials (or *discussion topics*) as a way of introducing new ideas.
4. Listen and learn from the group.
5. To use what was *working*.
6. Only tentatively approach *deeper* techniques.

I had two therapy groups: One met from 2:00-3:30 p.m. and the other met from 6:30-8:00 p.m. The members of the group consisted of convicts who were in prison because of forgery, burglary, murder, assault and battery, drugs, alcoholism, tax evasion, armed robbery (most)—some were *lifers.* The average age was thirty-two, with a range of education from the fifth grade to a B.S. from a leading university, with the average educational level at the tenth grade.

My groups were not the only ones in the state prison, but I was the only *outside consultant* specifically working in group therapy.

The group therapy *room* often changed. It was either located in one corner of a large, hard to hear room, which vibrated from the noise of convicts going up and down on iron stairways; or it was a hot, stuffy, small room located in the aisle of one of the cell blocks—referred to as the *chicken coop.*

The phases or *flow* of the groups will be divided into initial, middle, and final phases. There were, as could be surmised, no sharp divisions, but an *ebb and flow* into and out of these three phases.

INITIAL PHASES OF GROUP PSYCHOTHERAPY

⟨Initially, I simply stated that I was going to be honest and open with the group, and that I would expect the same from them. I assumed there weren't any prima donnas and I assured them I wouldn't be one. ⟩

After some initial hesitation at the first session, a discussion developed around, "It's more difficult on the streets than in here." The group divided itself fairly evenly; one side felt it was easier "on the streets," the other side held, "it's easier in here."

By the second group therapy session, I began to introduce *discussion topics.* I asked, "Would you rather be mentally ill or a convict?" To my surprise all preferred to be a convict. One stipulation was made—the crime should not be murder. Reasons advanced by the convicts for their choice were two:

1. "A convict's mind is O.K."
2. "A certain date and you're out."

This I felt was important information, and it proved helpful on many occasions.

In the next session I asked, "Which one of you is most mentally ill?" This brought a great deal of *bounce* to the group. There was considerable disagreement, and as comments were exchanged the group felt a *punch*.

In the course of the lively exchange the question of intelligence was raised; one member stating, "John is a crook who got caught because he's so stupid." The statement was made by Sam, a self-appointed leader, who seemed to be saying he wasn't fearful of any of this *stuff*. So I asked him to rate the smartest to the dumbest in the group. The group was involved! Angry accusations flew back and forth between various group members.

The question for discussion at the next group therapy session, was "whom does the average citizen prefer, the mental patient or the convict?" All felt that mental patients were preferred by the public because they weren't responsible, "They lost their marbles." Finally one convict stated, "We are the dregs of society." This so infuriated another inmate that a fight almost ensued, stopped in all likelihood because the angry inmate left the group. He returned the next week. This method, which might be termed *provoked discussion*, was a useful modality at involving the group, during which valuable information concerning themselves was released.

I should add a personal note. I began to experience frustrations I had not experienced in other settings; namely, the matter of *turn-outs*. If *by chance*, one of the group member's name was left off the list it was impossible to get him to the group. His name had to be on a twenty-four hour prior notice. The members sort of enjoyed my frustrations. They would say, "How would you like that for twenty-four hours a day, Doc?"

There were several expressions which the group used which I did not know. It was a delightful experience for them to *fill me in*. Some of the rather common terms were:

1. Big mover—upper class con. 2. Shank—knife. 3. Jacket hanger—jail label. 4. Bull—guard. 5. Shuck—to put on a front, to be fake. This is one of the most common expressions, as "Oh, he's just running a shuck." 6. Punk—a young convict, or a convict who will have sex in exchange for cigarettes or candy. 7. Jocker—a worn out punk waiting for revenge. 8. Twig—a mentally ill person. 9. Shoot a kite —send in a request for some favor. 10. A beef—any kind of disagree-

ment, why the convict is in prison, what he is legally charged with.
11. Bitched—a habitual criminal sentence. 12. Queer bread—french
toast.

In exchange, I would explain some of the common expressions
I used, as projection, denial, paranoid, masochistic, etc.

This *education-exchange* was a means of growing closer, of
becoming more acquainted—give and take.

Shortly, one of the group referred to another convict (not
in my group) as a *rat* as he ran *his case down*. I inquired if there
was a *rating* among prisoners. They quickly informed me: 1. First
rank (lowest)—is a rat (tells on others) 2. Second rank—raper
(who can also be a rat): a. incest b. child molester c. assaultive
raper d. garden variety 3. Third rank—fruits: a. Jail house—not
built that way, but will for cigarettes. b. Real homosexual 4. Agi-
tator—but "He'll put a jacket on you for going to AA, Chapel,
or group therapy." 5. Ding-a-ling—mentally ill. 6. A soild con is
honest—does his own time and own thinking; "suppose a fellow
borrows a free cigarette, he'll pay back, when he says so."

Group involvement took another turn, when I learned that the
group *(my men)* were given a *bad time* by some in the yard. The
yard is a large open space in which all the convicts meet for recreation. It was the group's estimation that, "70 percent of all
the cons don't go for anything—of this, one half would like to do
something to benefit themselves but they are afraid of the ridicule
from the rough ones. Of the 30 percent who go for help (whether
education, AA, group therapy, or whatever) about one-half are
sincere, the rest do it on a *shuck job*. Some of my group (half)
admitted that originally they came as a *shuck*, but they were
now *hooked*.

MIDDLE PHASE

[The group moved into the middle phase as members began to
look at themselves, began to reflect on their behavior.] Statements emerged: "I like a good time"; "I'm not backing off when
any dude says something to me"; "What the hell, I like women
and drinking, but I blow everything"; and, "I got balls on me,
they won't push me around." This last remark led me to make
the following statement: "John, you have one big ball—for fun

and raising hell, but you got an awfully little ball for responsibility, loyalty and work." This statement perhaps it was their language—or—it just made sense, had a terrific impact. The entire session revolved around, "How can I grow the other ball?" In fact, it has stayed with the group, and was frequently referred to time and again.

Intermingled with the above, some heated discussion emerged concerning loyalty to one's children. One of the group (Joe) insisted that he was loyal to his children, but the other members attacked him and a fist fight nearly ensued. Eventually, Joe had to agree that he wasn't really loyal to his children, otherwise he wouldn't be in prison. Many of the members remarked that they weren't even loyal to themselves, not to their *jail partner,* or *fall guy*—giving numerous instances of how this backfired.

As they began to wonder what kind of people they were, new *tools* were given. For instance, I utilized the concept of Wallace and Fogelson (1965) which suggested that there are four types or kinds of identity:

1. The feared self: a deep down feeling, that one might be insane or incurable, or a habitual criminal or lacking in normal intelligence, a homosexual, etc.
2. Ideal self: what one wishes he were, (It was remarked that some people feel they are what they wish).
3. Real identity what one really is.
4. Claimed identity: what one insists others say about him, or act towards him. It was indicated that this is often a source of trouble in the pen. For example, "I want others to think I'm a tough guy, while in fact I'm a coward." Toch (1969) treats this topic at length, using the phase *self preserving strategies,* that is, enhancing the individual's "ego in the eyes of himself and others." This could also be termed, *claimed identity,* or in convict language, *keeping on a good jacket.* This group was urged to translate the kind of courage needed in the joint, to the kind of courage needed in group. This thematic thread reappeared in several sessions.

Once again, the above affords a framework for a meaningful discussion and the group began to *check out* (ask others in the group) what other members thought.

(Individually, each member began to question himself—to put himself under observation.) Joe reflected, "I guess I've always wanted attention, to be the big shot. To spend money—." He then related an armed robbery, in which he pulled the trigger to kill a man, but luckily the pistol failed to fire. In another instance, he did shoot, but missed. I suggested that Joe *rob us*—the group; that he relive an armed robbery; that he go out of our group therapy room (the chicken coop), use a pencil for a gun, and rob us. There was some initial hesitation, but the group, now all in favor, insisted. Joe *robbed* us.

After the robbery drama was completed, I questioned Joe with the following hypothetical question, "Suppose the head shrinking business doesn't go very well and I get out of it, and my wife and I open a Ma & Pa grocery store. Some fifteen years from now, when I'm an old man, and you're out and in need of money, you rob our store. Then all of a sudden you realize, 'It's old doc'. What would happen?"

Joe said, "First of all, I wouldn't be robbing no little store." "Oh, but suppose you do," I insisted. Joe replied, "I'd just sorta leave." "What if I made a move?" "Then, Doc, I'd figure it was you or me, and I'd probably let you have it." "What? I replied.

The group began to vigorously disagree with Joe. A month or so later, Joe opened the group session with how stupid he felt in that "damn robbery act," as well as "what I said about killing Doc." He insisted that a change began at that time. Joe is now out of prison (eighteen months) and from all appearances seems to be making it.

This particular event triggered other group members. For instance, Hank opened his shirt, showed on his bare chest, numerous old wounds. He remarked, "I'd get on a drunk for four to five days, and I'd be so disgusted with myself, I couldn't get off it, want to fight someone, and if I couldn't find someone, I'd start cutting on myself." Bill exclaimed, "What!" Hank responded, "Up to now, I thought it was an attempt at suicide. It wasn't for sex, but to be close to my wife. She'd get on the phone and call my mother." Shaking his head, Hank sighed, "This impresses the hell out of me." Sam inquired, "Tell us some more about you and the wife." "My wife, she was a tom boy type and not affectionate and I wanted affection," replied Hank. From reports, I learn that Hank is out and doing well.

These two incidents prompted the group members to *search* themselves.

The following technique was utilized for further exploration. They were asked "which of your five senses, do you most appreciate?" As the members began to speculate on this question, the following statements emerged:

1. Sight, snap-shots, I look once, quick, and then look away, it tears me up.
2. I can look at snap shots and think of the good old days.
3. By looking at pictures, it is a way of getting out of the pen.
4. That old mess hall is hell, and I try to get two showers a week. So I tried to get a job that I could shower every day. I never worried about this on the streets, so I guess it's smell.
5. There is a stink in here. I guess I prefer smell-fresh bread cooking, for example, like when I was a boy . . .
6. I can't listen to good music, it reminds me of good sounds: memories are hooked up with it. 'My cup runneth over', I damn near cried and 'Harbor Lights'. It's one of my favorites, I'll start bull shitting to ignore it and not cry.
7. I miss smell of cosmetics, and the smell of a woman, smell of a brand new car, clover fields, pine trees.

Ray, moved by the momentum of the session related that he had malingered. He reported that he had been able to get by two psychiatric examiners, relating in detail some rather clever maneuvers. This so intrigued me that I asked if he would see me next week and put this on tape. He agreed and forty-five minutes were spent in taping. (See Appendix 1 for part of this taping.)

FINAL PHASE

The group now moved into a new phase. (This phase might be termed the *ego expanding* or *testing its insights and strengths.*) Earlier (by the second month) I had mentioned that it would be beneficial to have one or two guards sit in on the group since, so much of their conversations were directed against the guards. This idea was negatively received. Many of the group stating that they would leave the group if this happened. I mentioned this idea again. The idea now began to receive support. A few of the members recalled how a guard might be a pretty good guy at first, but slowly became embittered by what the convicts did to him.

Mike took a stand with me mentioning that "Lt. Jones would make a good one to bring to the group." All the group knew Lt. Jones and about half of the members agreed he was a good guy. Mike would ask Lt. Jones to come to our next group therapy session. Lt Jones came on his off time. The group functioned well, and the Lt. entered into the dialogue. At the close of the session, Lt. Jones said, "This is the most impressive experience in my twenty years at the pen."

It was so successful other group members took turns asking officers to come. At one session we had eight members and four guards. During this meeting the notion of a snitch emerged. One guard stated, "We never go and ask for information. That would make us look like a fool! What would one of you do to us?" Bob responded, "I've been in the joint for ten years and never thought of that." It was a revelation to all the convicts, the officers or guards never asked for information—it was volunteered.

Eventually, the convicts agreed they hang *jackets* on the guards. This point must be stressed because two months prior to starting the group, the prison had experienced a riot in which the convicts set a fire resulting in extreme financial loss. The feeling between the inmates and the guards was particularly *touchy* as a result of this, not to mention the friction which led to the riot. ⎧The group had now taken a significant step and it indicated to me a modification, or a lessening of one characteristic, which I think is frequently associated with criminals, namely their concern for justice for themselves but a radical ignoring of their actions (often unjust) to others. In their search for, or better still, their insistence on justice, the criminally prone individual is apt to become violent.

Toch (1969), in the foreword to his book, *VIOLENT MEN*, writes: inmates trust sctime guards etc.

> Violence, in our view, must not be circumscribed by legal or socio-economic classifications. It must be viewed in the context of taverns and school rooms, in prison cells and living rooms; it encompasses felons and police officers, inmates and guards, it covers brawls and killings, riots and revolts.

It is my observation that members of the group experienced

less tension and fewer occasions for violence as a result of group participation.

(Another modification of personality was also occurring—trust. The factor of trust is important and necessary in the healthy development of an individual.) The following, in my opinion, is an illustration of going from mistrust to trust:

1. In the first month the question of hypnosis arose. (I informed the group that I've often used hypnosis as one of my treatment modalities.)
2. Hypnotic induction techniques were employed but none of the group were able to be hypnotized—which I interpret as *being on guard*—not trusting.
3. Later (three months), hypnotic induction techniques were utilized and this time all the group could be relaxed (by a hypnosis method) and several of the members became good hypnotic subjects.

(This I think is an example of going from mistrust to trust) Convicts often find it difficult to put themselves in another's place. They appear to be so *glued* to their own positions. Hence, role reversal was a valuable therapeutic modality and I feel it should be included in all group therapies with convicts.

These considerations have led me to be attentive to the group's thinking. Beck (1967) writes, "These findings suggest that a thinking disorder may be common to all types of psychopathology." This interest of mine was related to the group and they engaged in talking about how they think. I have included a few examples, as illustrations:

1. Dave: Fake reality, if I build up an image of myself, like being a big mover then I have to live up to it; no one else believes in me, so I have to try and prove that I believe in myself.
2. Joe: I do a lot of angle shooting. I go up to someone and talk as though I'm really interested in him, but I'm merely setting him up!
3. John: I do time in the pen, by hate, on the outside I use gimmicks like alcohol—most of us are bored.
4. Jim: I was in a bubble, everything was going fine and when the bubble broke, I couldn't face reality.
5. Fred: Take this bad beef stuff. The con says he was driven into it by bad circumstances, so he's not responsible—so it's all

fixed up and now he looks good. In other words, he wants someone else to think it was a bad beef—he really doesn't.

6. Ben: Oh, we just forget what we do and blame it on others. I know a con who stole a car, had it for three years and when it was stolen from him, he forgot he stole it and reported it to the police and got caught for stealing it in the first place.

7. Ed: Just the other night, I heard of a couple of cons in their cells, talking about how to kidnap the Lennon Sisters and I listened to it—I began to think how I'd do it. Damn this is how we get into things.

8. John: (In Appendix #2 is part of a long written response given by John.)

Nine months after the group's existence, an all day seminar took place. It was a program on treatment for personnel working in the state's correctional institutions. Each correctional institution's director was present, as well as his treatment and counseling staff, in addition to Department of Vocational Rehabilitation personnel working in each state correctional institution. I was asked to participate. I replied, that for my part in the program I would like to bring some of my group to the seminar and demonstrate group therapy. This was agreed upon, but shortly it was decided that only those convicts who were on minimal custody would be permitted to attend since the seminar was located outside the penitentiary. This was awkward, but I still felt that a demonstration would be beneficial. An alternate plan was decided to have the two on minimal custody, plus two other inmates whom I did not know, join in and form a *demonstration group*.

After our participation, we received ample praise from the observers. It was felt by most present that group work did have a very useful part in the penitentiary's treatment program.

Two weeks later, one of the group members who had participated in the demonstration, reported to the group that he had an interesting customer at the Curio Shop. This store, which is located in front of the penitentiary, sells leather crafts and other products made by the inmates. Ben, our group member, stated that the interesting customer was a state legislator. Ben reported to the state legislator that group therapy was very beneficial and that some of the guards attended on their own time. This was a very generous gesture on Ben's part and was gratefully appreciated by the guards present in the group.

At one point (ten months after the group had been under way) a reporter was allowed to *sit in* on one group therapy session. His impressions appeared in the Oregonian, the State's largest newspaper. His comments were quite favorable, which is a needed type of publicity for the lay public. A favorable quote from the warden also appeared in the article, and this, too, was— and is— a benefit to treatment programs.

Other criteria suggest that the group had been rather successful:

1. None of the group landed in the hole.
2. None had bad write-ups.
3. None caused trouble.
4. Some of the reports concerning them, by guards had changed for the better.

It is far too early to talk of lasting results, but some indications begin to appear. Those who left the group on parole or those who *flattened* their time, have so far not returned to prison, and from all appearances seem to be making it.

Evaluation of my experience of therapy in prison is unlike Halleck's (1971) who questions ". . . whether I behaved morally in carrying out psychotherapy in prison at all." On the contrary, it is my impression that my participation of conducting psychotherapy in prison has enabled me to be a better advocate for improvement.

My judgment concerning the effectiveness of psychotherapy agrees with the findings of Carney. Carney (1971) in his study on the effectiveness of psychotherapy in a prison setting concluded that psychotherapy is markedly effective for some prisoners, namely:

1. Inmates with shorter records benefited most significantly.
2. Older inmates with longer records.
3. The longer these two types of inmates remained in treatment, the more the recidivism rate was lowered. Psychotherapy, however, did not benefit the ". . . younger inmate with longer records." In fact, the longer this type of inmate was involved in therapy, the higher the recidivism rate.

REFERENCES

1. Beck, A. T.: *Depression: Clinical, Experimental and Theoretical Aspects.* Hoeber Medical Division, New York, 1967.
2. Carey, F.: Evaluation of psychotherapy in a Maximum Security Prison. *Seminars in Psychiatry,* 3:363-375, 1971.
3. Halleck, S.: *The Politics of Therapy.* Science House, Inc., New York, 1971.
4. Toch, H. H.: *Violent Men.* Aldine, Chicago, 1969.
5. Wallace, A. and Fogelson, R.: Chapter X. In Boszormenyi-Nagy, I. and Framo, J. (Eds.): *Intensive Family Therapy.* Harper and Row, New York, 1965.

APPENDIX 1
Discussion with Ray

Dr. Scott: I want you to tell me a little bit of the particulars of that Ray — did you just wake up one morning and didn't know who you were or just cover it up.

Ray: What led up to it was that I had worked about thirty-six hours around-the-clock in the fire room punching water tubes, now this is where you go in with a long rod and knock the soot out. I had worked about thirty-six hours without let-up, not even a break and the reason was we had poor water and were low on power and there wasn't many men who could take it. But, to get out of this work, I just detested the work, not so much the work, but the guy standing over me while I was doing it and I just got where I hated those guys in the service, I really did, just like my stepdad — I hated them because they stood right over me and made me do things just like — all I could remember was my step-dad, you know it's a horrible thing to hate somebody like that. So I layed in my bunk and got to thinking about it, boy it had worked before, maybe if I pulled something like *I couldn't remember anything* and just forget where I am and who I am and really play it right down to the end. I had heard of guys doing this, getting out of the service, maybe it will work for me. So, I went out on the deck in the middle of the night and its just like here in the penitentiary — they have a count — they come around and count heads you see, make sure everybody is alright. Well they missed me and I wasn't on watch, so they thought I was overboard and I knew they were going to think this, so I went out and sat on one of these deals — I can't even remember the name of it now, but you take and turn the rope around it and tie the ship up, I sat down and just stared at the water and I knew what I was doing all the time. These guys came out and said, 'Hey, what are you doing sitting out here in the cold, bud?' I didn't answer them, I just didn't answer them. I didn't talk to anybody and they finally got two guys to pick me up and I went along with them and they steered me right into the hospital, right through a place where the aides were and they tried to talk to me and tried to get something out of me and the only thing I thought was that it may be good to kind of throw in 'who are you?', that's all I said. I really played it to the hilt. I thought this all out before I did it, so they took me over to the hospital at Sasebo, that's in Japan, and I spent three weeks there and I guess you might say 'under evaluation' if that's the word to use . . .

Dr. Scott: That's a good way to say it.

Ray: I couldn't remember my own mother, dad, the service, where I was, I didn't know who I was, who these people in the white jackets were, I didn't know why they were giving me shots, I'm not mad, I'm not doing anything wrong; in order to make this thing look good I decided to remember some things, so I went back to the card table, still, I didn't have it down pat, and someone asked me to play Pinochle. I said, 'Sure', sat down and started playing Pinochle. Then, they asked me where I learned to play Pinochle, I said, 'Boy, I really don't know,' and all of a sudden I knew I had made a boo boo. I knew I would have to do something to cover it up, so I layed in my rack and I never spoke to anybody all that day, or the next day. About three days went by and I never spoke to anybody, two days I wouldn't eat anything, wouldn't eat a bite, and finally I got up one morning and I said, 'Boy, I'm hungry', and looked around me and I said, 'Anybody got anything to eat?' Just like I was a normal human being, just like I knew where I was at, and so the guys brought me some chow and everything, came in and talked to me for a longtime, I just talked up a storm, just like nothing happened. Everything they wanted to hear I said, like 'You ever been in the service?'; 'I don't think so,' 'Where is home?' 'In the United States,' 'Where?', 'Oh, boy, I don't know.' Then during all this questioning, I acted like I was confused, and became confused. I couldn't get my mind to focus, I just couldn't think. So, I layed down on my bed in the afternoon, and what really set it off was when they brought me to Oakland Hospital in California.

Dr. Scott: All the way from Japan?

Ray: Yes. While I was laying on the rack I got to thinking. I got to do something, when the orderly came to give me a shot in the afternoon, I acted like I was sleeping with arms hanging over the bed. He came up to me and when he started to shake me I come out of that bed, really came out of it swinging, and I don't really think I hurt him very bad, I dived right out of that bed and through a plate glass window, just dived right through it. Well, a couple of the guards brought me right back and I knew what I was doing all the time. I wanted out of the service so bad at that time, I wish I could do it over again. They took me back inside and stripped me down. Maybe two to three hours after this happened, they put me in a Ward of some kind and I couldn't remember anything. Then things came back and I got a discharge, a general discharge, don't ask me how I got it, I don't know.

Dr. Scott: Were you seen by a psychiatrist or psychologist?

Ray: A psychiatrist saw me all the time.

Dr. Scott: Yes, but how did you go about fooling him?

Ray: I don't know, doctor, just the same general way; except I never acted the way the others did, I just played the role of not being able to remember; bits of my memory came back, like playing Pinochle and they'd ask me where I learned to play, and I'd say, 'Oh, my mom taught me,' then they'd say, 'where's mom?'. I really thought about everything before I answered the questions.

Dr. Scott: Did you watch anybody else there so you knew how to handle them?

Ray: Yes, I did but you remember earlier I said I knew other guys doing this before in the service. Well, I watched these guys. Some of the other guys that were doing the same thing I knew, they were because I was trying to get out myself, so I knew they were playing. But they acted one way and I didn't want to act that way. I just figured by golly, if they can fool them, I want to fool them that much more. I got one guy or a dozen guys I thought were acting (by pulling the not eating bit). If they wouldn't eat, then I'd eat like a horse, if some guy would walk up to them, they'd ignore them, then I would walk up to the same people, smile and say 'Hi, how are ya,' I really played it up, I think I did a fabulous acting job.

Dr. Scott: Then, you got out of the service . . .

Ray: Yeah, OK., then I got out of the service . . .

APPENDIX 2
The Character of Convict Thinking

The convict, is, above all else, egocentric. His thoughts and thus his actions, both conscious and unconscious, reflect a take all, give nothing self-centeredness. The basis for such a way of life is probably an overemphasis of material values. In reality, most convicts are imprisoned because of their dishonest pursuit of money or material goods.

Taking care of number one is where it's at, seems to be the general consensus hereabouts. The statement says one thing of the convict: he wants and will take, but he is unwilling to give.

A prison makes life within its walls a personal thing and perhaps the inmate can be excused, under the circumstances, for caring so exclusively about himself. Certainly there are good justifications for this attitude. For the time being, though, let's just accept egocentrism as part of the convict's repertoire and continue with it in mind.

The single most constant and important aspect of inmate

thought, call it deviant if you wish, is *negativism*. *Negativism* has permeated to some degree every convict in prison. If he doesn't already harbor a trace of negative thought upon entering the prison, he will be surrounded by it until he leaves. It's difficult to fight. If an inmate feels as some do — that constant pessimism and negative self-concepts lead to negative behavior — he tries to alter his thought patterns. He tries to think positively. And what happens?

First off, he's labeled as being naive and *square* for his inability to see and interpret what others see and interpret negatively. Prison officials and guards aren't much better examples of positive thinkers than other convicts. The negativism dwelling within these walls is immune to uniforms, age differences and social status. It strikes everyone, save the chaplains and they've probably had bouts with it.

Prison committees, and the reports these bodies base their findings on, are negative by nature. It's never *What has the convict done right lately*, rather it's *what has he done wrong lately?* So, the policies of the institution perpetuate negativism as well.

Negativism is firmly entrenched in prison and there are undoubtedly several more causes for its continued presence. Those who find themselves in prison are, after all, losers of some sort. For one reason or another, they have attempted theft, rape, murder or whatever, and lost. They were caught and here they are, ostensibly to pay for their indiscretions, rehabilitate and go back again and function normally in society. But wait!

Not too long after he's in prison, he'll find that prison isn't a panacea for society's ills, that it's not helping very many and that in fact it's hurting most. He'll find, too, that he cannot depend on staff members to do what they say they'll do. He may be placed in some kind of vocational training program and then taken out and placed in some other job for the convenience of the institution.

Should he be interested in improving his education, he might be assigned to school where there are no provision for pay or good time. So, as he attends school and learns and smokes Bull Durham, his next door neighbor shakes shit out of sheets at the laundry thereby earning $.50 a day and smokes Camels. Where are the incentives to interest convicts in learning, which is certainly a more rehabilitative calling than separating sheets? Where, indeed, are the institution's values? It seems the prison is more interested in making what money they can from an industrial laundry operation than in doing him some good.

So, we can justify a large portion of an inmate's negative or pessimistic attitudes and lay them on the doorstep of his environment. Add to this the rampant negative reactions of those he talks to each day, the sardonic, satiric prison humor which, for the most part, takes form in negative beginnings, and have a negatively-oriented person. His negativism is reinforced constantly and he in turn bombards others with it. Where does it end? It doesn't because there's more.

The convict, by tradition, has been one of the lowest creatures in the human social system. Many convicts still believe in this very tradition and express desires of being nothing more than a *good convict*. And what exactly is a *good convict?* He is an ignorant fellow whose image in prison is more important than anything else. To enhance his good con facade, he talks to guards and prison officials only when absolutely necessary. He presents officialdom with the image of an uncooperative convict. He will not take an order without gesturing or voicing annoyance, nor does he permit prison routine to function smoothly if he can alter matters. He tries to keep the keepers in a state of disruption.

He's not a snitch; he hates rapos and child molesters. He's proud of his activities, or lack of them, and he's proud, too, that he's a good con. His self-image is self-defeating and negative. He's at the lowest level of society; he's expected to act untrustworthy, secretive, surly and uncommunicative. If not, why all the guards, guns and locked doors and constant petty harrassment?

Further, he is subjected to a system of which he wants no part and a system in which he has absolutely no voice. The officials paint a false picture of prison. How else, pray tell, under these circumstances, is a convict supposed to think? Positively! I have yet to meet a convict in this prison who does not harbor a hate for the prison and its officials. They won't always be open and honest about their thoughts when facing staff members or guards, but in every convict, of common intelligence, there resides an intense hate of everything conected with prisons. And no one who has not done time, can ever know to any great degree what it is to be a convict.

So, the convict feels everyone connected with and working in the prison is against him. Maybe not against him personally, but against him as a convict. His only salvation is to get out of prison, get away from the source of all the hate, confusion and fanatic adherence to rules and regulations that foster the negative environment. And when he does get away, he hopes he can stay away.

The Convict and the Square John

If we can take one individual, say a married man of thirty-five years with three kids, a mortgage on a $20,000 home, two cars in the garage and an executive position, let's call him a fair representative of society. Here, then, in the convict vernacular is the *square John*. He's got more going for him that most cons will ever have. He's probably got some education, he's getting a fair wage, he's accumulated property and a family — in short, he has most things some cons will never have. And, we'll assume he's obtained them honestly.

But he's the enemy, and a complacent one at that. He'll pick up his paper and read and believe what prison officials tell reporters about how wonderful convicts are treated and what great rehabilitation programs are carried out at the pen. He'll go on to the sports page with a smug knowledge that he's part of a humane community that pays for and, by God gets, progressive penology. He looks at his wife and says, "Things must be going well out at the pen, they haven't had a disturbance there for fifteen years," and that's just the point.

The square John, doesn't care or even particularly want to know what goes on in prison as long as there are no riots. Because of his apathetic nature, prisons are run under a curtain of secrecy. Officials are choosy about who enter and why. There are forms and paper work prior to any special visits and they consume time and take patience. If and when visitors are finally admitted, they are entrusted to some official and are escorted on a *Cook's Tour* and shown the finer points of a humane penal operation. Very few get a chance to speak to prisoners, and those that do are always in the presence of an official. Are the visitors escorted to the Segregation and Isolation Building and shown how prisoners are stripped and left in a cell with little to eat for days and sometimes weeks? Hell no! They walk by on the outside and it is pointed out to them and they'r told they can not enter for their own safety. And they, for the most part, accept the explanation.

Then comes a riot, and our citizen taxpayer is outraged at the audacity of those convicts who just fired three million dollars worth of buildings and disrupted such a progressive penal program. Now he is mad and he demands as a taxpayer that something be done. And so it is. A grand jury is impaneled, a few convicts tried and sent to other prisons, a warden is replaced, a corrections director fired. The taxpayer is satisfied. He goes back to his newspaper and he won't be heard of again until some more buildings are burned or a few people shot or maybe some ex-convict steals his car or burglarizes his house.

The convict knows and contemplates this inactive citizen. He knows no one cares how this place is run as long as riots are held in check. The square John doesn't care about the con, so the con doesn't care about him.

A convict doesn't feel any loyalty or compassion for a society which places him in prison and forgets him. The con may not try to hurt that society, but neither will he consciously help it.

CHAPTER IX

CONFLICTS

Stanley T. Tyler

THE REHABILITATION OF a convict begins with an emotionally shattering experience and gradually dissipates in an adaptation to a new life style. Its effectiveness is determined by the events which happen in the interim and how the person interprets these events. My beginning point was arrest. At that time I believed that rehabilitation was a mystical event occurring within the walls of a penal institution.

My concepts of the inner feelings of a convict were based on what I had previously heard and imagined. I found these concepts conflicting to what I experienced. My experiences began on January 16, 1964 as I sat in my home drinking coffee. Eight detectives came to the door with a search warrant which listed items identified in recent burglaries. I stood speechless, looking at my wife. Helplessness and fear welled up in her and her eyes began to moisten. In a moment many things went through my mind but not a word would come from my mouth. The police turned my house upside down and I stood there impotent and immobile. I wanted to blurt out all kinds of explanations to my wife but the look on her face told me that she was near panic. She had suspected for some time that I was involved in something illegal but had repressed her suspicions because they were too painful. She looked as if the whole world had come to an end. Neither of us could speak.

When the search was completed I was informed of my rights and taken into custody. Knowing your rights and being able to act on them at this point are quite separate. I was aware of what I had done but I was not sure how much the police knew. In the hours that followed the detectives put me through many interrogation sessions. I am not being judgmental of the techniques used. However, in my confused state, I was incapable of exercising my rights to legal counsel. When the police presented what appeared to be enough evidence to attain a conviction regardless of what I said or did I signed a confession. I felt that if the police believed I was being cooperative my punishment would somehow be less severe. When I did receive counsel I was told that if there was any doubt about my guilt I had removed it all by my confession. This left me with resentment and bitterness toward police which was to last for many years.

My next two weeks were spent in the county jail. In my bewildered state I kept expecting to awaken and realize it was all a bad dream.

The shock back to reality came one morning when I was called out of my cell. My insides did a turn and left me with a sensation of fear unlike any I had ever known. It was the day of my trial. Pats on the back and wishes of good luck from fellow prisoners did nothing for me as I left the jail. As I walked to the court-house I felt as if I had already been tried and convicted. I was like a man at the top of a ladder and each thing that began to happen to me took me down a step.

With a prior police record and a signed confession my trial was very brief. The fear in me mounted as the attorneys talked about me.

I felt like saying "This isn't me. I'm not like that at all." I was trembling slightly as I stood before the bench and received a sentence of ten years in the state penitentiary. My heart began to pound with the fall of that little wooden hammer and the sheriff's hand on my shoulder. I could not speak. I was choked by a lump in my throat and I seemed to be looking through a puddle of water. I swallowed hard as I walked from the courtroom. I had lost my freedom and taken the first step down the ladder.

Outside the courtroom I was shaking all over. A man whom I had known in the community came and took my hand to say good-bye. I could not speak so I just nodded my head to my last friend and took another step down the ladder.

I returned to my cell in complete shock. Someone asked how it went and as I opened my mouth to speak I broke down. I was hurt and feeling sorry for myself. This was the release of all the fear and anxiety that had built up in those two long weeks after my arrest.

I was called from my cell again. This time I really had to fight with myself to answer. I had not wanted to face my trial and I knew this would be much worse. I stepped through the door of the visiting room and saw all four of my children looking at me with their eyes of innocence. How could a man explain this to four small children who still think you are the greatest guy in the world? What impressions of value could I leave with a six-year-old boy, or with the others who were younger and could not possibly understand? The only thing they understood was they were losing their dad. I did not know what to say. I had practiced something but it did not seem to fit. They surrounded me and each one hugged and kissed me. I had to say something fast, I only had a few minutes. I looked at my wife for some sign of help. The look she returned was empty. It was as though she was still bewildered but now there was a shield around her that would not let anymore hurt penetrate. I swallowed the lump in my throat and turned to my oldest son. Tears were in his eyes as my shaky voice broke the awesome silence. "Do you remember how I used to scold you when you were naughty," I began.

He nodded but did not speak.

"Well, that is how Daddy used to punish you. Now I have done something naughty and I have to go away and be punished by living in a prison."

He said, "I know, Mommy told me."

The tears started to edge out of their containers and trickle down his cheeks. I tried to swallow and began again, "I'm going to do the best I can to hurry back to you."

I felt a gentle tap on my shoulder as the deputy motioned for me to break it up. I turned back to my children and was again surrounded and embraced. This time I felt the trembling of their little bodies as they fought back their sobs. I stood up and hurried from sight as my own cheeks moistened and again the pressure oozed out in a release of sobs.

"Oh, God, how much of this can one man bear?" I prayed to myself. I had been cut off from my family and taken another step down the ladder.

This was the beginning of my rehabilitation. I was not yet at the bottom of the ladder but this series of events was an important part of my motivation for rehabilitation. These events were also completely foreign to anything I could have imagined or prepared for.

The actual ride to the penitentiary went by so fast that I could hardly believe it when we arrived at the gate. There were questions on my mind that created a fear and this was not the only time I was to be aware of them. Later in my rehabilitation they would recur and be just as frustrating. I pondered such questions as: What would it be like there? Would it be as tough as I had heard? What if I did not fit in? Would I get pushed around? Was my family as frightened as I? What did they think of me now? Do they think I have done this to hurt them?

As we entered the building I began to tell myself: "I'm going to live here. I have no choice. I can adjust to this. I'll just mind my own business."

I began to learn I had very little business and what I had would be minded by someone else.

It is difficult to put into words how I felt entering prison. I was about halfway down the ladder and I was holding on to each step with a thread of hope that somehow circumstances would change and the process would stop. Then, as I faced each encounter I was forced down a rung at a time.

I was taken into a small room and stripped of my possessions, my clothes, my pride and what was left of my self-respect. Now I was really beaten. How can a man fight for his right to be treated like a human being when he is standing there with nothing to fight with but the button God gave him, and right then he is not even sure of it's creator! Had I sinned against society so greatly that I deserved this? What else could they possibly think of doing to me? I learned not to ask that last question, even to myself. It always seemed as if they heard me and then showed me.

My clothes were returned momentarily so I could be taken to the hospital for a physical examination. They were taken away again in the shower room where I was stripped naked so a guard could look down my throat and up my rectum to see if I had smuggled in any drugs. I took a shower and put on my prison denims. I was taken for a haircut and had my fingerprints recorded. Just prior to visiting the world's worst photographer, I remember thinking they could make the most pleasant person look as if he was angry at everything that ever lived or moved.

A fear lingered in me and I did not want to speak. I just wanted to try to feel out the whole situation. It was as if I were floating on a very feeble raft. If I made no waves I could stay on the surface.

As I was taken from place to place I would pass other inmates. Some would nod and others would just look. I felt like I was in no-man's land. Legally I was a convict but I did not seem to fit with these men. If I happened to be where one would feel like speaking he would ask three questions which made me feel more out of place: "What are you in for? Where did you fall from? How much time did you bring with you?"

I started doing things instinctively. They put food in front of me and I ate it. I was not hungry but I wanted to do everything right. I did not want to make waves. I had been told of an isolation period when I would be in a cell separated from everyone for twenty-one days. I wondered what that would be like. I was afraid that I could not make it without losing my sanity. I did not have long to worry before I was taken to my cell. I experienced the sound of the locking of a steel door. I had heard it before but not with this finality. All of the fears of my entire life seemed to hit me at once. My legs began to tremble and I quickly sat down on the steel rack that hung from the wall. This was the first time in fourteen days that I had been alone. Thoughts began to leap through my mind. I had really done it this time. I did not think I could handle this. I had gotten myself in too deep. I had always been so smart about getting out of jams. How could I get out of this one? I could not. I knew damn well that I could not. I was the master of hurting people. I had never done anything right.

I began to speak out loud to myself. "I chose a good wife. Lord! look what I have done to her. She sure must be proud of me now. Then there is my mother. I've hurt her so many times."

Then came a brainstorm which recurred over and over again during the first months of my sentence. I could kill myself. I guess the reason I never did, was that I was looking for something good about myself. Suicide would have proved that I was a coward as well as being rotten. I had always believed prisons were full of hardened criminals. I certainly would have changed the public image if they could have seen me sitting there talking to myself and coming apart inside.

I cleaned my cell and picked up the brown sack I had been carrying. It contained everything I owned. I had a carton of cigarettes, a ticket that said I had three dollars in the office and two pictures. I looked for a long time at the pictures. They were of four children and their father, or at least the father they had had. I felt my eyes burn with tears as I remembered that last trembling moment when I held them in my arms. I settled back on my bunk swallowing hard to hold back the sobs. "Oh God, please help me through this long, long night!"

In the days that followed I became more and more mentally disturbed. I received no mail from home and this produced a fear that I was losing my family for good. Eventually the day came when I received a letter severing my family ties. This was the bottom rung of the ladder. I know now how low a man can feel.

I must step out of this experience to explain that I have not contradicted myself as it may appear. I have stated that this was all part of my rehabilitation. Thus far, it appears that it has been debilitating. Let me assure the reader that my life to this point had been a demonstration of gross inability to adapt to society. I had filled a reservoir with mechanisms of manipulation which were destroying me. The events I have described did nothing more than empty this reservoir so it might be refilled with more constructive mechanisms. I had, in actuality, been going through a dissocialization process where I was banished from the society in which I had demonstrated an inability to live. In my opinion, this was the value of sending me to prison. I was not sent to a particular place where something painful was inflicted upon me for punishment. The punishment was the process of being cut off from the most widely organized group of persons with common goals and ideas which were similar to those I had set for myself. As my ties to the society outside were cut off, I was forced into a society inside the walls that I was sure I did not belong in. I found I had to live within the rules of this new group if I was to survive.

With this decision I began my adjustment to prison life. A feeling of wanting to belong somewhere helped the adjustment. When I would question if I was really a criminal or when some incident happened that I refused to identify with, my adjustment would falter. It always seemed to come back because of my need to be accepted.

Living in an institution of a thousand or more inmates is frightening. Following the line of least resistance, I found it much easier to initially attach myself to a small group of inmates. They provided me with the basic ground rules and at the same time supplied a certain amount of protection from the total prison population. This group was as close as I could come to calling any of the inmates friends.

During my first six months I struggled desperately to hang on to two values, I felt were helping me to remain a part of society outside and at the same time doing what I had to do to be accepted by the inmates. Vocational training and schooling were the two things I worked hard at.

If I were asked by a counselor or supervisor why this was important to me I always stated "It will help me when I leave."

If a fellow inmate asked me why I was being such a *brown nose* I said, "I'm shooting an angle for an early parole."

I guess it was the deviancy in my intent that made it acceptable to the inmates. I found many of their attitudes to be of a rebellious nature against the society which had banished them. Guards, work supervisors, and other institutional staff represented the society outside and were automatically a source of ill feeling. Close relationships with staff were dangerous, and yet a certain amount of feeling was necessary to solicit favorable reports. I came to like a few staff members quite well but I never stepped beyond the acceptable guidelines.

After isolation I was depressed for several weeks. The inmates refer to this period as *pulling hard time*. I was really trying to decide if it was worth all the struggle or if I should kill myself. I had never been able to live within society's rules and I could see no means of being assured that I could change. At this point I was still pretty much a loner in prison. I had not tried to enter into any close relationship with anyone because I was afraid of getting involved with homosexuals and those who drank or used drugs. When you eliminate these people there are few left. However, I did not want any close friends. Each man has his own problems to deal with and I did not want to be exposed to anyone else's problems.

There are a few rules in prison society which are of particular importance. A man's number and sentence are his personal identity. Any action which brings this number into unfavorable attention to the officials or would adversely affect his sentence is grounds for reciprocal action. The worst such action is *finking* or *squealing* on another inmate. The punishment for this can be anywhere from a mild beating to death depending on the recipient and the seriousness of the action taken against the other person. Once branded as a *fink* acceptance in the prison society is impossible. Most new inmates are tested when they enter prison. After the inmates are sure you can be trusted you are left alone to learn the few lesser rules such as not incurring a debt beyond your means of paying off.

As I stabilized myself mentally I became aware of the dissocialization process that had taken place as I entered the penitentiary. It was evident that a reintegration process would have to take place when I left the prison if I was to be successfully rehabilitated. Before release I had to learn to live within the rules. There were several areas where this could be learned in prison but not all were satisfactory. Some types of behavior were acceptable to the staff but looked upon unfavorably by the inmates. For example, I tried singing in the choir. I may have scored some *brownie points* with a few staff but I could feel a large number of inmates looking critically at me. An activity on the other extreme was gambling. The inmates were perfectly willing to accept this behavior but the staff looked critically at it. In the middle were activities such as baseball, horseshoes or any hobby. The one I found rewarding for myself was that of writing articles for the prison magazine.

The activity I could most closely relate to a similar situation outside was the pay system. For each day I worked, a certain amount of money was recorded in my account in the finance office. Once a week I could apply for a book of tickets which could be spent at the canteen. I found it very similar to a checking account. I never borrowed from anyone and I lived within my income.

I had been able to maintain a few ties outside the prison. My wife would occasionally write about the children, but my mother and sister wrote very infrequently. These letters had a marked affect on my moods. Often they were encouraging and made me feel better but occasionally one would throw me into a tailspin of remorse and depression. I would have trouble sleeping at night and would lie awake thinking of the mistakes I had made. Then I would rebuke myself for being so stupid. When I did sleep I would dream of losing my wife to another man. This was somehow the maximum threat to my masculinity.

It seemed to trouble me at times that I was projecting one image of myself to the inmates and another image to the staff. An important step in my rehabilitation came when I entered into a continuous relationship with myself. I felt that if I could be honest with myself in this relationship it would help me keep this kind of role-playing from becoming my reality. The interesting part came when I realized these images were all slowly merging into one consistent image which became what I wanted to be. With the help of my counselor in group therapy and individual counseling, my life began to take on meaning. The months went by and I began to look forward to the future.

I decided that another try at reconciliation with my family was worthwhile. I began with a letter to a minister, whom I had never met. I asked him to call on my wife and see if he could counsel with her. He wrote stating that he would be at the prison to visit me in a few days and would give me a report. When he came he brought my wife and children with him. She had also decided to try once more. These were my first ties back with society and the first two steps of the reintegration process.

Reintegration is a matter of plugging back into the elements in society which were unplugged during dissocialization. I had to look at my elements very carefully. I felt each one had to be compatible with the rest if I was to be successful. I began to see how this had been a problem in my life before and I wanted to find new elements to plug into where the previous elements had been conflicting. One such factor I recognized, was the group of friends with whom I drank. Since I now believed that I had a drinking problem I did not want to return to this group. I began to look more seriously at Alcoholics Anonymous to replace them. I found Alcoholics Anonymous to be a group which accepted me unquestioningly without judgment of my former lack of insight.

Reintegration is a much slower process than dissocialization. There seemed to be a conflict in the penal system which was disruptive to the process for me. I started to become aware of this toward the conclusion of my incarceration. My high school education was complete and my teachers felt I had done a good job. I had completed my vocational training and my supervisor felt I was ready for competitive employment. My counselor felt I had made the necessary adjustments in my life to successfully function in society but I could not be released. These people, who were in charge of my rehabilitation, had no authority over my sentence. The Board of Parole was the only authority which could grant me the opportunity of leaving the institution. I could feel myself becoming bitter as I began to look at how the system functioned. It did not seem to matter what I had accomplished during my incarceration. More emphasis was placed on the length of time I must be incarcerated for the particular crime I had committed. I began to see where murderers and rapists had to stay incarcerated much longer than I. It was not that it took them longer to rehabilitate but because their crime was more morally repulsive to society. At this point rehabilitation lost its effectiveness for me and the whole penal system became an aversive process. I could feel myself becoming bitter and resentful. My last four months in prison came very close to destroying everything that the first fourteen months had accomplished. It is impossible for me to project how long it would have taken for this aversive process to have a permanently damaging affect on my rehabilitation. I can only say it was there and I was beginning to feel it.

The Board of Parole did grant me a parole after eighteen months in prison. I accepted it as a reward for the work I had done while there. It was not presented to me in that way. If I had accepted it in the manner it was presented it would have been another aversive condition. I was told that my parole was an implement by which the State could control my rehabilitation and return me for further punishment at anytime they felt I needed it. Before I left prison I felt the Parole Board really wanted to punish me. At that time if I had done what I believed they wanted of me I would have committed another crime and been returned. I was determined to rebel against their wishes. I was bitter at the whole system from the judge through the lowest security guard. I was even bitter at the whole society which instituted such an unreasonable system.

When I went out the prison gate I was frightened. Many of my fears were created by questions which were similar to those I had when I entered: What would it be like out there? Would it be as tough as I had heard? What if I did not fit in? Would I get pushed around? Was my family as frightened as I? What do they think of me now? Do you think I will hurt them again?

Adjusting to life outside of prison was much the same as adjusting inside. I sought out a clique or group where I was accepted and had some protection. I chose Alcoholics Anonymous. I was comfortable there and it seemed that the more I talked about how bad I was the more they accepted me.

My family ties were well established now, and I began to work at putting new support into the other social elements of my life. My employer and the chief of police became two of my best supporters. I do not think it is so important who I received my social support from but it had to be there. The bitterness I held toward the Parole Board almost destroyed me. I have always believed that my parole officer understood my feelings. He told me when my parole started that if I filed my reports and stayed out of trouble I would seldom see him. The day he handed me my release papers, we were equally satisfied about the lack of contact we had. If he had not held this attitude the chances of my succeeding on parole would have been questionable.

It would seem that this would conclude my rehabilitation, but the ending was not to come until June 10, 1969 on the fourth anniversary of my release from prison. I was sitting in a room full of therapists as a part of my training at the State University as a counselor. I had just told the group that four years ago I had been released from prison. In the preceding four years I had often exposed myself as a recovered alcoholic and an ex-convict. I had also related my bitterness toward the Board of Parole.

On this particular day one of the therapists hotly retorted "What in the hell is that to us?"

I was stunned and became immediately defensive.

"Well it means something to me," I replied. "I think I've come a long way."

"I believe you're a loser," he snapped back.

Now I was so god damned mad I could not speak.

He leaned forward and spoke directly into my face. "You're stuck in a role. You've got yourself in a box and you can never get what you want until you let go."

Perhaps it was the bewilderment on my face that made him continue because I could not reply.

"You tell the world that you're an alcoholic and a convict and as long as you don't drink or steal, who can say anything bad about you? You're safe as hell. I'll tell you this much, as long as you throw that in people's faces you'll never be placed in a position of responsibility where you handle other people's lives or money. I would never want to employ you until you let go of that role and be whatever you can be on your own merit."

I sat speechless but my mind was spinning like a top. Could he be right? Was I afraid to let go of my role and forget my bitterness? Is that how people really saw me? I felt as though he had just opened a new world to me and removed the shackles so I could enter it freely. This was really the change of attitude that completed my rehabilitation. As long as society could clearly see what I had been I was not rehabilitated. Only when I could no longer be identified as someone odd or different was the process finished.

SECTION FOUR
OUTSIDE THE WALLS

CHAPTER X

COMMUNITY CENTERED TREATMENT OF OFFENDERS

GORDON BIRD

RECENTLY IN THE United States, considerable conflict has been generated around the rehabilitation of the public offender. Significant tragedies occurring within the penal system during 1971, including the fatal shooting of an inmate at California's Soledad Prison, and the deaths of a number of prisoners and guards at the Attica State Prison in New York, have compelled the public to become painfully aware of the immense failure of the nation's prison system. This chapter will focus on a recent alternative to incarceration of felons in large correctional institutions—the community treatment center. Sometimes identified as work release centers, these facilities seem, to many workers in the field of corrections, to offer considerable hope in the rehabilitation of offenders.

Our effort here will be to explore briefly the reasoning behind the development of community treatment centers and to provide some descriptive material relating to their development. The major part of this chapter's concern will be to describe a relatively typical community treatment center—the Milwaukee Work Release Center. I am currently working in this program as a vocational rehabilitation counselor.

Ramsay Clark (1970) succinctly explains the need for this type of special facility. Clark wrote:

127

The most important statistic of all in the field of criminal justice is the one which tells us that probably four out of five of all felonies are committed by repeaters—that 80 percent of all serious crime is committed by people convicted of crime before.

Unfortunately, the average citizen is unaware of the futility of confining a convicted criminal in a maximum security custodial facility such as a penitentiary. Nor is the uninformed taxpayer cognizant of the tremendous cost of maintaining a person in this type of institution. Torok (1971) indicates, that, "On the average, it costs $6,000 per year to confine an inmate in a state prison or reformatory. This figure includes operating and often hidden capital expenses."

A more serious concern of our citizenry should be the irrelevancy of our prison system in relation to the demands of society at the time the offender is released back into the community. Keller and Alper (1970) state:

> The experience of passing an extensive period of time within an institution inevitably fades out many patterns of conduct brought from the outside and replaces them with newly acquired modes of behavior . . . the establishing of more complex patterns of behavior brings with it a related concern—how persons who have had their lives planned for them for some considerable period, will deal constructively with the leisure which will fill at least two thirds of their time, assuming a normal work week. This host of problems (which many persons who have not been in correctional situations may never master) adds up to a total burden which not all newly released offenders can be expected to carry without help.

The inability of some offenders to maintain an adequate adjustment in the community is another important reason for the community centered treatment facilities to be helpful. The offender's access to experience and practice in coping with problems he will face upon his return to society can make a significant difference in his ultimate adjustment. Therefore, it is imperative that the person be furnished with an environment which provides appropriate controls, but also promotes sufficient flexibility and scope for personal development in problem solving.

The enormous costs of imprisonment, high recidivism rates,

and the inability of the institution to teach constructive behavior has provided some of the impetus for the establishment of the first work release facility in 1965. Prisoners selected for this type of release were able to work in the community for an understanding employer during the day and spend evenings in nearby jail facilities. Competition was keen for the available employment. The success of this initial experiment has resulted in a considerable expansion of the concept of work release; halfway houses, prerelease centers. Community treatment centers are becoming the major thrust in a number of state correctional systems. The most recent focus has been on increasing the individual's responsible behavior in the community, assisting him with complex treatment modalities.

I have been associated with one of these community treatment centers since March of 1970. The Milwaukie Work Release Center, the first to be established in Oregon, currently is serving as a model for an expanding system of transitional services for the offender. Four new centers have been opened throughout the state in recent months, and this trend is expected to continue.

The Milwaukie center is located in Milwaukie, Oregon, a small urban community adjacent to Portland, the largest city in Oregon. This facility is jointly operated by the Oregon Division of Corrections and the Vocational Rehabilitation Division. The center itself is situated on the banks of a small creek. The facility occupies approximately five acres of parkland. The center is somewhat isolated from proximity to residential housing; at the same time, it is still relatively convenient to local businesses, bus lines, and recreational facilities.

This center accepts men from the Oregon State Penitentiary and the Oregon State Correctional Institution, both located in Salem, Oregon's capital, about forty-five miles south of Milwaukie. The men are carefully screened and, wherever possible, are transferred to the Milwaukie facility approximately six months prior to the time they would normally be discharged outright or released on parole.

This particular work release facility has the capacity to house forty-six men in approximately 4,400 square feet of space. There are two large dormitory units containing bunk beds, with adjoining space for personal belongings. In addition, there is office space for managerial and counseling staff, a kitchen, and laundry and washroom facilities. A large central area is utilized as a dining area, it doubles as a general day room for the men to watch television, play cards, or visit friends and relatives.

In contrast to the penitentiary, with its emphasis on locked doors and barred windows, the doors at the Milwaukie center are never locked. There are no bars on the windows. Movements of the enrollees to and from the center are monitored by custodial personnel on an around-the-clock basis. Men could easily leave the center at any time by exiting through the back door. During the initial few months of the center's operation, there was a relatively high incidence of men absconding, but the number of residents leaving has diminished considerably. Now a runaway from the center is a rarity.

This center is unique in that it functions also as an educational release type of facility. One third of the resident population is in attendance at some type of school. In addition, services can be provided to assist in the development of work skills and habits for selected individuals.

Personnel at the Milwaukie facility are supplied jointly by the Corrections Division and the Vocational Rehabilitation Division. The center itself is administered by a Corrections Division manager, who coordinates the efforts of six assistant managers, along with two cooks and their helpers. Assistant managers are responsible for checking the enrollees in and out of the unit. They also issue short-term passes and carry out a number of other duties related to the movements of the men.

The Corrections Division employs a person who is designated as the work release representative. He maintains contacts between the center and the man's employer or related school officials. He is responsible for fiscal matters relating to the enrollees. The men turn over all of their checks to their representative, who deposits this money to the individual's work release trust account. From this account money can be judiciously withdrawn to provide for the man's transportation, clothing, and incidental expenses. The Corrections Division withdraws sufficient funds from the man's account to pay his monthly room and board bill.

One of the purposes of work release is to ensure the person of adequate financing when he discharges. Rather than the $100 provided by the state, the person on work release can leave the center relatively solvent. Many of the men are discharged from the center with savings averaging $500; some have left with as much as $1,500. This *nest egg* can help the man considerably when he reenters the community.

The work release representative approves passes for the men which are in excess of four hours duration. Provided a man's initial behavior at the center is appropriate, he can be granted a twelve hour pass each weekend in addition to his four hour passes during the week. If his subsequent actions reflect an awareness and a positive response to the regulations set by the center, the person can increase his weekend passes to two. Ultimately he may be allowed overnight passes in the community.

The Vocational Rehabilitation Division currently maintains a staff of five at the center, including two rehabilitations counselors, a job development specialist, a secretary, and a counselor aide. This staff is intensely involved in vocational counseling and related planning for the men, additionally it provides educational and vocational evaluation as well as seeking appropriate job placements and providing therapeutic activities such as individual and group counseling. It has been necessary for the Division to supply transportation in many instances and to provide assistance for medical or dental problems. Financial assistance is provided for students in the form of payment of tuition, books and supplies, transportation, clothing costs, and incidental expenses, while they attend school. The Vocational Rehabilitation Division also retains a part-time psychiatric consultant whose function is to guide the activities of the total staff so that inappropriate behavior can be dealt with more adequately. He may interview some enrollees when conditions warrant, or he may spend his time instructing the combined staff on effective means of working with the residents. These consultation sessions provide valuable learning experiences for both staff and enrollees. This resource has helped the Milwaukie center to make significant progress in the development of a treatment program.

In conjunction with the overall treatment goals of the center, group therapy is provided by a psychologist retained by the Vocational Rehabilitation Division. The two rehabilitations counselors also lead two additional counseling groups, so that there are four therapy sessions each week.

The role of this particular work-educational release center is to provide guidance and direction for the men in their attempts to make satisfactory adjustments back into the community. Convicts released from the prison may have no employment readily available and they frequently have not acquired the necessary work skills which industry demands. Perhaps the point was well made by one former resident of the Milwaukie center who commented, when experiencing problems, that he might as well return to the penitentiary where he would not have to face so many problems.

The ex-felon has to make many adjustments when he steps outside the door of the institution.

In order to meet the need for and the benefits to be gained from specialized treatment facilities for criminal offenders, an adequate personality description of the man entering the Milwaukie center is necessary to help tailor his treatment modality. There is a persistent tendency for the men to be labeled in the penitentiary as suffering from a character disorder with anti-social features. In addition, slightly over half of these men have an additional problem of either alcohol or drug addiction. This diagnostic label as suggested by Abrahamson (1950):

> is reserved for individuals who are basically unsocialized and whose behavior pattern brings them repeatedly into conflict with society. They are incapable of significant loyalty to individuals, groups, or social values. They are grossly selfish, callous, irresponsible, impulsive, and unable to feel guilt or to learn from experience and punishment. Frustration tolerance is low. They tend to blame others or offer plausible explanations for their behavior.

Abrahamson writes, "Psychiatric-psychological studies indicate that a large number of prisoners are emotionally or mentally disturbed." He further suggests that imprisonment without psychiatric treatment does nothing for the individual as far as altering his basic personality pattern, and the person continues to commit crimes. Most prisons are poorly staffed with the kinds of personnel who could help the individual with his underlying problems. Again, Abrahamson states:

> Examination of the records of prisoners show that only 20 to 25 percent are dangerous and therefore in need of confinement in a maximum security prison . . . if all prisoners were psychiatrically examined and classified, the remaining seventy-five percent might well be placed in a rehabilitation center instead, where they would be treated and reeducated by individual and group therapy, according to their specific needs, until they could be returned to society.

The Milwaukie center has operated it's treatment program along guidelines similar to those suggested by Dr. Abrahamson, yet other factors are also important. As a rule, the institutional prisoner was furnished with few opportunities for constructive decision making while he remained incarcerated. The community treatment center, conversely, strives to supply controlled experiences relating to decision making which take into account the particular individual's capacity for decisions at that moment in time. Utilizing this method in a controlled milieu will provide better opportunities for the individual to learn and to personally develop.

To facilitate the emphasis on maturation and personal development, it is necessary to delineate subgoals which will provide a framework for the individual in making his choices, and this in turn assists the staff in evaluating the man's progress while in the center. These subgoals reflect a progression through five interrelated stages; movement from one stage to another does not necessarily occur smoothly and rhythmically.

OBJECTIVES FOR PERSONAL DEVELOPMENT

The first goal of such a program is to assist a person by providing him with the opportunity to make a satisfactory adjustment within the center; he needs to learn how to accept and how to function with authority, instead of resisting authority. This initial step is necessary for continued progress in an individual. He must learn to obey center rules, just as he must obey the laws set down by the community. Prisoners in my experience appear to have considerable disdain for prison regulations. They tend to make a game of *putting-one-over* on their keepers. Most of the men need special help in adjusting to different rules and regulations. The granting of increasingly greater responsibility, along with greater freedom, can help the individual to become more motivated towards improved behavior.

A second subgoal of the Milwaukie program is related to obeying laws and regulations. It is necessary for the individual to acquire or develop adequate inner controls. Development of these controls enables the man to participate more effectively in the program at the center, as well as other living or working situations, which are, or will be, appropriate to him as an individual. In order for the person to internalize these newly presented controls, he must have opportunities to learn and understand the consequences of his own irresponsible behavior.

A third aim is to help the person to develop more constructive means of coping with reality. One means of learning how to deal with reality is to be faced with it in a manner which is not devaluing or destructive. The staff helps the resident in learning more about his personality through group psychotherapy. Abilities are more adequately identified through psychological testing. Intellectual functioning is also assessed and this information is interpreted to the client. Helping the person in making more realistic choices concerning his future, not only in personal matters, but also in vocational problems, is of considerable significance in future adjustment.

Fourthly, the Milwaukie center assists the individual in developing genuine feelings of self-worth. Generally, the large penal institution tends to utilize negative approaches in it's dealing with a prisoner emphasizing his detrimental qualites, or focusing on the terrible crime he has committed. This approach is minimized at Milwaukee, and generally speaking, the man is rewarded for his good behavior by being granted extra privileges. A conscious effort is made by staff to socially reward positive behavior by means of commending him verbally or giving him a pat on the back. At the same time, inappropriate behavior is not dwelt on or overemphasized to the exclusion of other considerations. An effort is made to deal with negative behavior in a manner which will help the person to look at his behavior and to make his own adjustments, perhaps even prescribing his own consequences. In this way, more effective learning takes place. The man takes responsibility for his own actions, and in so doing, increases his feelings of self-worth. The individual is less prone to put the blame for his actions on someone else.

Finally, an effort is made to help the person to use his potentialities in the community in an effective manner. Community participation is encouraged wherever possible. The staff of the center allow residents as much time in the community as they can *handle*. Emphasis is on gradual community participation, since the individual will have to function on his own in the community relatively soon. Experiencing the community will undoubtedly aid the man when he is discharged. At that time the individual must be prepared to make his own decisions, where will he live, whether or not he will seek a new kind of employment, and how he is going to maintain himself in his personal relationships.

To facilitate some of these goals, the Milwaukie center has developed some unique features designed to aid the enrollees in their social and emotional growth. The various facets of the program being described represent a flexible, changeable program. Hopefully some of this flexibility will be emulated by the enrollees, and will form a part of their future repertoire of behaviors.

One means of assisting the enrollee in making more appropriate decisions is to limit the number of available choices on his arrival at the center. The man basically is restricted to the center for the first week and leaves unaccompanied only when going to work or school. At other times he is accompanied by a staff member or the correctional aide. This method allows the staff the opportunity to observe the individual and to evaluate his reactions to new situations and to the rules and regulations imposed on him at the center.

After a week's time, the enrollee is allowed to leave the center on a social pass for four hours a day, and for twelve hours on the weekend. If he is able to handle this freedom satisfactorily, he is gradually given more responsibility in the form of additional twelve-hour passes, then occasional overnight passes, and finally home leaves of longer duration.

He is accountable for keeping his sleeping area clean and neat and must return to the center from school or employment within the allotted time. As the individual develops more responsible behavior, he is rewarded by extended time in the community.

When the enrollee abuses these privileges by returning late from a pass, drinking while on pass, or breaking other work release rules, he is brought before the unit team for disciplinary action. The unit team consists of the center manager, the work release representative, the rehabilitation counselor, and counselor aide. Although the counselor aide has no vote, he does have a voice in the decisions, since he is generally more cognizant of the man's attitude. The unit team listens to the enrollee's explanation. Appropriate action is taken, depending on the circumstances. The team may recommend no action be taken or may restrict the man's passes for one or two weeks. In more severe cases the team recommends return to the penitentiary. In this way the man knows what he has done wrong, has a chance to present his own case, but more important, he has the opportunity to learn from his experience in a positive way. It is important that the person should, wherever possible, be able to indicate to staff his version of what happened. Sometimes the person cannot accept the fact that he had done wrong and so continues to defy or break the same rule, or a different one, at the first opportunity. In such a situation, he might receive a substantial restriction, as well as being warned that future negative activities of this nature would result in his return to the penitentiary.

The unit team deals with other infractions such as fighting in the dorms or drinking on the premises. Fortunately, these incidents are now extremely rare. Since almost half of the men are taking Antabuse while at the center, drinking has been dealt with more severely by the unit team.

Special programs have been set up for those who have drinking problems or for those who have experienced difficulties with drugs. Generally persons referred to the center suffer from more severe emotional problems. Individuals who have resorted to excessive use of alcohol are supplied with Antabuse in pill or liquid form on a daily basis. This method is intended only as a temporary crutch; however, it is an effective crutch. In most cases, more effective means of coping with life's problems can be incorporated into the individual's behaviors. The man, having experienced sobriety and it's related success for at least a short time, tends to develop a more healthy perspective.

Some difficulties emerge with the use of Antabuse. For example, a few of those taking Antabuse have managed to avoid ingesting the pill by placing it under their tongue and later spitting it out. Although there has been some abuse of alcohol at the center, drinking has not been a significant problem.

About 10 percent of the center's population are persons who have experienced problems relating to narcotic abuse. A portion of this group is placed at the center on a drug surveillance program. Once a week, on a random basis, these individuals are required to provide a urine sample, which will be analyzed to determine if the person has been taking narcotics or dangerous drugs. The opportunities for drug usage by the individuals is severely limited while on the program because the sampling is randomly done.

Other drug users, who have elected to take Methadone at the Alcohol and Drug Center, state operated, also receive periodic urine analysis. Methadone is a synthetic narcotic which can be allocated in individually controlled doses. This drug seems to alleviate the psychological craving for *hard* narcotics. Unfortunately, in our experience, Methadone has not proven to be a satisfactory solution for the enrollee with a drug problem. One of it's disadvantages has been that it seems to reduce the person's vocational adjustment to a considerable degree. Seven men have been on Methadone since the opening of the Milwaukie center and not one has made a satisfactory work adjustment, either while on the program or after discharge. Some noticeable side effects have been observed, such as *nodding*, (going to sleep while working) as well as emotional variations effecting his ability to adjust to those around him. Our experience seems to indicate a preference for the drug surveillance type of program for the drug user.

Another unique feature of the Milwaukie center is the utilization of one enrollee as a correctional aide in the center. Chosen on an experimental basis at the penitentiary, this man serves as a liaison person between the staff and enrollees. This innovative concept arose indirectly as a result of one of our group therapy sessions (Chapter XI). Several advantages are apparent with the utilization of this aide:

1. He can provide an orientation to the center for the new enrollees.
2. Generally the aide is the first person to become aware that one of his fellow enrollees is experiencing some difficulties in adjustment at the center, and he attempts to aid in the man's adjustment.
3. In situations where the problem is extreme or could be better handled by another person, he would seek their assistance. He is not meant to be a *snitch* or an informer, as his effectiveness would diminish considerably if this were the case.
4. He can serve as a liaison between enrollees and staff.
5. In unit team meetings he does not carry a vote but generally represents his fellow enrollee and voices opinions as to the appropriateness of various actions as they relate to the individual's difficulties.
6. The staff has the opportunity in the correctional aide's case to properly evaluate his abilities in constructively working with this population and also with people in general. He simultaneously advances his education through part-time attendance in university classes.

Another innovation has been the development of a house advisory committee, which has as its principle function the making recommendations to staff concerning improvements at the center. From time to time there have been matters such as meals, lunches, use and abuse of the telephone, money, hours at which passes should end and also physical improvements in the center, which have concerned committee members.

Very recently, the committee was restructured, and its functions reconstituted. The committee now consists of five enrollees, including the counselor aide. It takes more responsibility regarding the behavior of the men in the center. The committee considers initial requests for privileges, including extended passes and early discharges. The staff generally accepts the recommendations of the house committee. Although it has been a recent innovation, the committee seems to exert considerable influence in averting negative behavior on the part of enrollees. Staff have been required to meet only minimally for disciplinary purposes since the committee reorganized.

Another unique aspect of the program is the flexibility the staff has in helping in the area of work. Satisfying employment is felt by many to be a significant variable in the rehabilitation of offenders. It is advantageous that the rehabilitation counselor can, where appropriate, remove a person from a work program and provide him with carefully selected training, even though the initial purpose of the man's placement at the center was to provide him employment. Although there is a *job-finder* at the center, it is not always possible to find suitable employment without first providing the enrollee with a vocational skill or trade. Short-term training can be provided in these instances. Occasionally men are placed in on-the-job training, where an employer is willing to provide initial training for the individual. In such situations, the employer receives remuneration for the time he spends in training the man.

Conversely, it sometimes becomes necessary to remove a student from his school program when he shows evidence of failing or disinterest. Occasionally his program can be adjusted so he can enter employment immediately.

Vocational training utilizing local community colleges, is the most common form of schooling. The men average about six months in the center, and those in school generally complete only a portion of their total program while at the center. Some have already completed a considerable number of credit hours while in the institution, and can reduce their training time accordingly. Efforts to obtain further financial aid, after they leave the center, have been partially successful, and a number have been able to complete their training. Contact is maintained with the enrollees after they are discharged and Vocational Rehabilitation continues to assist in appropriate ways until suitable employment is obtained for these students.

In the field of rehabilitation, there is a strong tendency for counselors to attempt to fit the individual with a job in which he can most effectively function. Currently, high unemployment impairs progress in achieving satisfactory aims in this regard. As a result, we are forced at times, to make less than adequate placements. The individual is encouraged, once temporary employment has been found, to seek more meaningful work related to his interests and aptitudes. He can request assistance from the employment specialist. A variety of tools is utilized for aiding the man in planning for his future, such as psychological testing for job preferences, abilities and intellectual functioning, along with work tryouts, etc. Many times psychological information about the man's personality structure helps to evaluate his employability and to predict how he is apt to function on a particular job.

Another important key to an individual's success in the community is his attitude, both toward the community and toward himself. Considerable importance is therefore placed on the provision of group and individual psychotherapy for center residents. Since this aspect of our program is covered in much more detail in Chapter XI, my comments will be brief and somewhat pointed in nature.

Group psychotherapy is the treatment of choice because of budget and staff limitations. It is apparent that individual counseling can be a valuable adjunct to group therapy, and we are now becoming more skillful and sensitive in determining at what point individual treatment is pertinent. Many times a man may have problems or feelings which have never been discussed with another person, and the emotions related to these feelings are blocking the individual from further emotional growth. In such cases, a private psychologist is retained to help the individual work through these feelings. Many of those who have received this additional treatment seem to react more appropriately in the community, without continually being influenced by their negative emotions.

Currently, attendance at group therapy is a requirement, if a man is to enter the Milwaukie center. He may elect to go to another center where therapy is not required if he so wishes. There is initial resistance to therapy, and a considerable amount of staff effort is expanded in dealing with this resistance. It seems important to develop a nucleus of motivated enrollees who can have a pronounced influence on the more resistive clients. The resisters often become more positively oriented once they observe a fellow enrollee intensely involved and progressing in the sessions.

Another important consideration is that not every therapist can work effectively with convicts in a group therapy. Many men seem to be more concerned about not violating the convict code; that is, not revealing weaknesses or real feelings. This kind of resistance requires patience and long-term development of trust and openness amongst the enrollees before any real gains can be made with them in therapy.

During some initial group sessions, tape recordings were made of the interchange between the therapist and the men. Later, at their request, these tapes were played back to the men individually. Video taping has also been attempted on one occasion, but the high cost of maintaining such a tool does not currently justify this use on a more permanent basis, even though it has considerable potential as a treatment modality.

The Milwaukie Work Release Center has functioned for almost two years as a cooperative program, jointly operated by the Corrections Division and the Division of Vocational Rehabilitation. Yet, the aims of these two agencies appear incongruous. The Corrections Division seems to be historically and legislatively fixed on maintaining the custody aspect of the program. At the same time, Vocational Rehabilitation is more concerned with assisting the person to achieve his maximum independence. Somehow it does not seem compatible for the rehabilitation counselor to encourage the enrollee toward independent functioning, responsible behavior, and making his own decisions, when the custodial supervisor is emphasizing the importance of the man obeying his supervisor's orders, in effect, fostering the man's dependence upon the center. The situation indicated above is exaggerated, but does serve to point out the inconsistency of the roles of the two agencies. With this variance in basic philosophy, there has been a tendency towards mistrust and disagreement between the two divisions. A more mutually satisfying relationship is developing pertinent to the goals of both agencies. Simultaneously, the goals of growth and development within the clients is being fostered as staff of both agencies learn to work together more harmoniously. Even with this gradual blending of philosophies into a more workable program there are still differences remaining, limiting the effectiveness of the program. Notwithstanding this, we believe that tremendous progress has been made in our program in the brief time since the center began operation. The learning which occurred at Milwaukie has been applied to other new centers as they are developed in new communities.

RESULTS OF THE MILWAUKIE PROGRAM

Table I.
Period: March 26, 1970 to January 31, 1972

Total number of clients served by Vocational Rehabilitation	222
Less clients returned to institution for medical, other reason	11
Actual clients served	211
Clients failing on program because of rules violation, escape	80
Clients failing because of new crimes while at center	4
Clients failing because of new crimes after discharge	10
Total number of failures	94
Total remaining in the community as of January 31, 1972	117
Percentage of success	55.5
Percentage of failure	44.5
Average number of days successes were on program	110.4
Average number of days failures were on program	73.5

When one considers the failure rate for the correctional system as a whole as approximating 75 percent, it would appear that the Milwaukie program has effected a significant decrease in the recidivism rate of these offenders. It would also appear that there is some relationship between the length of the man's stay at the center, that is the longer the man remains in the program, the better his chances for success.

The reader should also remember that the majority of those being sent to the Milwaukie center are persons who have had significant problems in making adjustments in the community. These are not just the first time offenders, but in most cases are persons who suffer from more serious problems relating to drinking or drug abuse, which have been significant handicaps in their lives; others were arm robbery offenders—for extended periods of their lives, some were in prison because of murder.

Some of those who were returned to the penitentiary for rules violations have now been released from incarceration on a discharge basis. A number of these seem to be making better adjustments than previously when in the community. One continual lawbreaker has maintained a job for some nine months without assistance; in the past he had never remained on any one job for longer than two or three months at a time.

Although the concept of work release sounds hopeful, there

are discouragements and failures. Sometimes an individual in whom the staff has had high hopes has to be sent back to the parent institution for serious violation of rules. One man who was returned wrote to me immediately following his arrival back at the institution. He says:

> I am certain you understand how difficult it is for me to write, but I feel I should make an attempt. I know that the faith you had placed in me as a sincere and honest person must be completely shattered. I realize there is very little I can say in regards to my drunken and childish behavior of last Sunday night, but I feel I must make the attempt however feeble and futile it may be. To just say that I am sorry and ashamed would be a gross understatement, yet I am sorry and terribly ashamed of myself. I am ashamed because I let you down—I let Dr. Scott down—I let Carolyn down and in the final analysis I have let myself down. You three people had faith in me and I am ashamed because I didn't live up to your expectations.
>
> I don't know what to attribute my insanity to—the temporary loss of my goals and my golden opportunity. I did the very thing I couldn't and shouldn't do—I lost my head—I quit taking the Antabuse—I thought I could manage my affairs without the aid of a medical crutch and, yet, as I sit here in my cell writing to you I can plainly see that throwing away that crutch was and is the reason for my downfall . . . I had a golden opportunity—the chance to begin living a meaningful and constructive life—and not only for me but eventually the chance for helping others who have fallen into the same circumstances as myself. The loss of this opportunity is one of the hardest blows of all . . .
>
> I truly regret the actions that led to me being put back in the penitentiary.

Sometimes a person has to be returned to reality before he can take an important step forward with regard to a life style, an identity. This man, although talented and intelligent, could not, in my estimation, visualize himself in the position of being a helping person. Consequently he reverted back to the only kind of behavior he had known in the past—negative behavior. I believe it will take time for him to accept himself more realistically. It may happen that he will see himself differently in a day or a month, or perhaps after a year. The time for this person to be rehabilitated will come. When a counselor feels he understands the struggles occurring within an individual, it helps tremendously to ease the frustration and disappointment when failure comes.

Another former enrollee writes concerning his experiences with work release:

> As an enrollee of the work release program, I feel that my present situation is the best recommendation I can give to the program.
>
> I am a college student in my sophomore year, a husband, an employee who pays conscientious attention to the duties and responsibilities of my job, and generally speaking a responsible citizen.
>
> From the time I was approximately fourteen years to age twenty-four my life was a series of failures. I left school at age fifteen, was involved in several encounters with the police as a juvenile, began drinking excessively at about age seventeen, unsuccessfully embarked on a career in the Navy, was married and divorced in less than eighteen months; finally my failures culminated in the commission of a felony and being sent to the correctional institution.
>
> I realized that my lack of education would be a considerable barrier for the rest of my life so I began attending classes at the institution and acquired my high school diploma. When I finally became an enrollee in the work release program, it was understood that I would continue my education on the college level; and I was sent to a housing facility in Portland.
>
> Many people ask why a convict can be a model prisoner while in an institution but as soon as he is returned to society he immediately falls back into his old patterns and becomes a burden to society. I can speak only for myself in attempting to answer this, but I know that most of my reactions to everyday problems were immature attempts to deal with life situations I was not prepared for; for instance, quitting school at an early age because I wanted to do something else; not being able to deal with the service and its regimentation; failing in marriage; and having a disregard for authority and law and placing myself above the restrictions that laws place on everyone. In short, I had failed to grow up. Somewhere in my life my maturation had not kept pace with my physical growth and I had become psychologically unbalanced.
>
> In work release I was technically a member of society once more and through group therapy was given support in facing all of these new responsibilities.

Work release is not the entire answer to a convict's problems, however, it does give him the opportunity to begin living a life of some worth, while he begins to cope with the many difficulties he must face. Today I am living a more worthwhile and successful life; I must attribute at least the beginning of all this to work release.

This client continues to receive help while he is on parole in the community. He, along with others who have been discharged from the center, attends group therapy sessions on a weekly basis. This man seems to exemplify the problems which are faced continually by ex-offenders in the community. Continuing help is a necessary prerequisite for this group of people to be independent and successful outside of the penitentiary.

Developing facilities to help the offender in the community is not an easy task but one requiring complicated, sophisticated examination of the forces which tend to exert their influence in the community. Setting up these resources for our clientele has been an exhilarating and rewarding experience, while at times it is frustrating and discouraging. When investments are made in individuals and for some reason failure occurs, then one feels disappointment. There is positive progress in most instances.

Community treatment is here to stay. Even with failures, this approach is a viable alternative to institutionalization. To be most effective the correctional system needs to develop a variety of resources which will meet the offender's needs and facilitate positive development in the person. The community treatment center appears to be the type of resource which can best be utilized by an individual who can function relatively well in the community with some supervision and control, without resorting to crime as a means of support or satisfaction.

Just as there is a need for a specialized type of facility to deal with dangerous offenders, it is necessary to provide a variety of resources to serve those people who are not dangerous in the community. Some of these might function well on parole; others would benefit from direct return to their community with no supervision. It is important for the community as a whole to be aware of the need for differential treatment of offenders through a variety of resources and experiences geared to individual needs. Community treatment of offenders through the work-educational release program is one modern approach which will continue to exert a more positive influence in the rehabilitation of criminals.

REFERENCES

Abrahamson, D.: *The Psychology of Crime*, Columbia University, 1960.

Clark, R.: *Crime in America*, New York, Simon and Schuster, New York, 1970.

Keller, J., Jr., and Alper, B.: *Halfway Houses; Community Centered Treatment and Correction*. Heath Levington Books, Lexington, 1970.

Torok, L.: A convict looks at crime and criminals. *Catholic Viewpoints*, 27:17, 1971.

CHAPTER XI

GROUP THERAPY WITH CONVICTS ON WORK-RELEASE

EDWARD M. SCOTT

T HE FORMER ATTORNEY General of the United States, Ramsey
Clark (1970) noted that *hard timers* (those who favor long
penitentiary sentences) attacked the work-release program au-
thorized by Congress in 1965.

My efforts in this chapter will focus on group therapy for
convicts in a work-release program. The location and description
of the center, as well as the population has been amply and adequately described in Chapter X.

When contacted to conduct group therapy for this population,
I insisted that the group therapy sessions be held in my office
in downtown Portland. The rationale for this stipulation was:

1. A better setting.
2. It would afford a kind of *proving ground,* around which I hoped to
   develop trust and loyalty among the group members, as well as
   with me.

A brief mention of some reality factors will indicate some
hurdles. The center, for instance, would change its policy concerning attendance at the group—at times attendance was mandatory, at other times, it was voluntary. Second, there was a
constant change in group members. Third, the differences of
opinion between the staff at the center and myself concerning
particular convicts was at times a vexing problem.

I had two groups (one mandatory and one voluntary). Both

groups met on Saturdays at my office; each group had 1½ hour sessions, followed by *posting* for ½ hour with a Division of Vocational Rehabilitation employee (Author of Chapter X). The *posting* served three purposes:

1. In-service training for DVR personnel.
2. Discussion of the session
3. Emergency or special need for a particular member, if this was needed.

My therapeutic approach was a rather frank, open, realistic one. I felt these men could not be *conned* by mere techniques. Although this chapter will describe techniques and modalities utilized during three years, the underlying assumption is that a *man-to-man* relationship is pivotal. Near the end of this chapter, additional remarks concerning the kind or type of therapy employed, will be mentioned.

I made two other assumptions, both of which I think were therapeutic. I assured the group that they could say exactly how they felt, without any fear of retaliation—nothing went into their *jacket* (or file). I, also, could say whatever I felt. This, I thought would allow them to disagree with an authority-figure, without fear. It was my feeling that they had never experienced differences—and still remain friendly with the person.

Second, I never read anything from their *jacket*—hence I had a fresh orientation. I informed them of this and for a time they couldn't believe it.

With these realistic factors serving as a kind of background, as well as a brief explanation of my *therapeutic stance* I will direct my efforts at presenting group therapy as such with convicts on work-release.

The explanations will be divided into initial, middle and final phases.

INITIAL PHASE

Almost from the very beginning (two weeks after group therapy was begun) the group was in trouble with the center—three of the group returned late to the center. They had been drinking, they were *busted*—sent back to prison.

Now the group organized around:

1. A dislike for the correctional staff at the center.
2. Projection and rationalization were rampant.

Typically the sessions began with complaints, or just *plain bitching* by the various members. At first, I attempted to eliminate the complaining. I gradually became aware that it was part of their therapy, that is, group was a place in which they could air their feelings. During these *airings* the point was made that even on work-release they were not trusted, but rather treated as though they were in prison.

Several times the opinion was voiced, "Let's face it, we're in the Joint." They asked, "What do we have to do to be trusted?" When I countered with, "What kind of signals do you send out?" They were puzzled. I explained, that when a person is angry— he doubles his fists or uses violent language; if a person is happy, he laughs or smiles. As you might well guess, we never did arrive at any such simple answer regarding signals of trust, as compared to the signals for anger or fear, etc.; but it was (and is) a new concept against which to struggle. Most of the group said they didn't trust anyone. They felt it started from their parents and extended to their partner (or fall guy) who *ratted on me* and so mistrust continued to grow. They didn't trust, but they insisted that they be trusted!

At times members of the group (those in the mandatory group) questioned the benefit of group therapy. The following is a recorded group dialogue:

Joe: It's no good—I won't cooperate in group.
Ron: Group is no good.
Joe: What would a good group therapy session be like?
Dr. Scott: For one thing, you can be out front with me and not get into trouble, and I'll be out front with you.
Joe: Really? It won't go in my Jacket?
Dr. Scott: Right. But I don't want you belly-aching about me.
Joe: I never do.
Dr. Scott: You belly-ached about one of the officers at the center.
Joe: I'm *not* a snitch—no one, no S.O.B. can say that.
Pat: I've heard it said.
Joe: *What?* How dare any S.O.B. say that! You're lying.
Pat: No.

Jim: I've heard it.
Joe: What! (yells) Not in twenty years in the Joint—did I hear this!
Dr. Scott: But you have, here, in group therapy.

During the following week, Joe attempted to organize members of the group against me. It didn't work. In a short time, Joe got drunk, and was sent back to prison.

In the beginning phase, I utilized, more than in later phases, a kind of educational approach. I will only indicate a few brief topics employed by this method:

1. MacLean's (1964) discussion of the three brains of man, with special emphasis, that the old brain (or reptilian) brain, ". . . is not a very good brain for facing new situations."

I pointed out, that in the Joint, the old brain was sufficient, but outside (on the *streets*—at work, at leisure) the neocortex (new brain) is needed. The midbrain is the center of emotions. It was interesting to watch the reactions of the members to this type of information—and their efforts to use it. Humorous incidents occurred from time to time. As an illustration, I told Floyd to "use your neocortex this coming week." Floyd was supposed to give an example to the group at our next session of using his neocortex. Floyd began, the following week to relate an example of using his neocortex, "Ya, Doc, I did use my neocotex"—laughter burst out. We had a good time.

2. Some of the notions of Skinner (1971) met with extreme reactions; as illustrated by:

Jerry: That guy is nuts.
Chuck: I can't take it.
Al: With no feelings, you can't be honorable.
Bob: I just don't believe him. I wouldn't want to be alive, with no feelings, just a robot.
Harry: He's telling it like it is. At least we should hear more. I've got to understand things like this, before I reject it.

I pointed out, that much of their conversation in group was an effort to improve their environment. This produced a kind of shock and a fruitful discussion insued.

3. Beck (1967) on the strength of his research, as well as that of other investigators wrote, "These findings suggest that a thinking disorder may be common to all type of psychopathology."

During the group sessions, members were often challenged concerning their thought processes—or *how* they thought. Paranoid themes were the most frequent thought patterns, followed by rigidity, superificiality, and deviousness. They typically employed a *double standard*. I mean, they felt free to generalize about others ("all the cons are—; none of the bulls were—," etc.) but they wanted to be seen as unique and individual. They hated being *lumped* ("All you cons—").

Lastly, it seems as though a special kind of thinking emerged. It goes something like this: They figure (*reason*) they would not get caught *this* time, which defiies the rules of probability; that is, one's chance diminish as the risk increases. For instance, in Russian roulette, the more a person escapes, his probability of *getting it* increases. A sample of group discussion on this topic is as follows:

Harvey:	I know it, but the excitement was more important.
Chuck:	I felt I was going for one robbery and it was going to be the *last* one; and at times I didn't care if I got caught. I wanted off the booze and dope—I guess I was looking for help.
Joe:	Outwitting the establishment!
Dr. Scott:	Kind of like a modern Robin Hood?
Joe:	No, Robin Hood had his men. I worked alone.
Dr. Scott:	So, then a lonely Robin Hood.
Joe:	No.
Bill:	The cops could have been the king's men.
Joe:	Probably. They played at it. When I got it done—I'd giggle to myself, "You're okay."
Dan:	It's not like Robin Hood, but Bonnie and Clyde.
Fred:	No—but take this guy B. D. Cooper—who got away sticking up the air lines and parachuting. The public gave him support, even a professional person did.
Dr. Scott:	So, the emotional factors are most important, than reason, or the rules of logic?
Joe:	Ya—you put aside the rules of logic and are willing to go against the odds.
Bob:	Ya—it's the excitement.
John:	No—for me it was money. It looked like a good thing. It looked sure—it's a way to make a living and if I got caught, I'd get caught. I was willing to gamble—I just wanted to score big one time.

So, in summary, the typical convict doesn't follow the rules of logic. He violates them either for: (1) emotional factors, namely excitement or (2) willing to take the odds—to strike it rich, just once.

See Appendix 1, as an example of a group member's verbatum account regarding group therapy and thinking.

MIDDLE PHASE

The middle phase of group therapy centered around personal vignettes, dreams, questioning of the self, doubts and fears, value of crime, awareness of choices, and the reality of work.

A question the members often wrestled with was the difference between *having guts* and *having backbone*. The following is a recorded discussion of the problem:

Henry:	I've got backbone.
Jim:	Sometimes I think I got both, and at times neither.
Pete:	I don't have any backbone—if I did, I wouldn't have come to group
John:	You have backbone.
Pete:	I don't. You live to your principles. The reason I don't have backbone is that I *want* this—*Now,* so my principles go.
Jim:	Well, as I see it, I could be loyal to a job, not a wife.
Joe:	To stay out of the Joint, a guy needs backbone.
Dr. Scott:	How do you get backbone?
Pete:	Accept responsibilities. But how?
Roger:	Just put it there.
Pete:	Just change all my weaknesses?
Roger:	No, a little at a time
Pete:	Ya, I want to do something—to prove to myself—not to others!
Jim:	I see you as having backbone.
Pete:	No—I've fooled you *again!*
Jim:	You've changing. You're honest.
Pete:	Okay. I said, the other day, all my life, I knew *what's right* and *what's wrong.* Here—at my age, I'm stumbling through life. I used to have stomach cramps, at night, in the Joint, that would rip me up—not now, since I'm out. When I was in the Marines I had 'em. It happens when I'm in trouble! Wow! Wait! A guy who'd k ll like I did. In the Joint I thought of suicide. I hated the Bulls, the death penalty, one way to get killed, is to kill

a Bull—if the time in the Joint got too tough—I'd have a way out, for several years I felt that way; but I'd back off—this Bull isn't worth it, and I kept a *little hope.* When I was in the hole, it was bad; after seven days in the hole, I'd try to push everything out, if I thought of good things, I'd get depressed. I'd lose myself—where I'd been and what I'd like to do, and think of the happy times. I'd think of what I do when out of the hole—play basketball and I'd say, "I can't make it—I'll get a Bull and they'll kill me—I hoped; when the State voted against the death penalty, it really bothered me. (See Appendix 2, for a discussion of capital punishment).

Dr. Scott: Loyal to people and not principles.

Pete: Exactly. Principles don't pat you on the back—people do.

Dr. Scott: You can't pat yourself on the back?

Pete: Right!

To indicate the different level of discussion, the other group (the group that didn't want to come to group therapy) had the following discussion about the same topic:

Joe: I've lived by principles—not to snitch, and I've lived by by that code.

Dr. Scott: Is that your most important value?

Joe: When I was a kid, I had to.

Dr. Scott: Still a kid?

Bob: Not the most important, but it's a rule.

Ron: It says, "Mind your own business."

Ernie: "Keep your mouth shut."

Joe: In the Pen, you've *got* to live that way.

Pat: No—in the Pen, there's lots of stool pidgeons.

Dr. Scott: Do you guys sn'tch on the guards?

Joe: No, good God! (Angry)

Dr. Scott: If you didn't—don't get so angry. Do you fear snitches most, in the Joint?

Joe: Ya—

Bob: A snitch is a snitch.

Ron: A snitch is no good.

Dr. Scott: How could you guys snitch on me?

Ron: Talking behind your back.

Dr. Scott: I suppose you do?

Pat: I don't. If I get into trouble—why should everyone have to pay for it.

Ernie: None of us stick together.

An adherence to a code, seems to prevail instead of looking at the *code* or principle and examining it.

An avenue employed by some convicts is fantasy. At times, as a beneficial avenue, and at times as an avenue to more trouble and turmoil. Numerous examples emerged in group therapy; perhaps the following two examples serve as useful illustrations.

One member, Louie, reported that his girl friend *broke off*. Louie felt this as a *blow*, since he was on Antabuse, he couldn't escape by drink. He decided to pretend he was in a movie, ". . . playing a part"; and this helped to *soften the blow*.

Another member of the group, Stan related:

> I had confidence in my ability to lie, and thereby live a life of fantasy. I was in Alaska, broke. I began to drink one night at the bar, and got to telling how much money I was making. Later, I got to thinking, if I have all this money, why not write a check. So I did. I flew back to Portland and wrote more checks".

> I used a weak spot in people. If people come into contact with confidence, they felt it and I took advantage of it. If they thought I had money, they'd fall all over themselves. I began to have an infallible sense about this.

Dr. Scott:	That's pretty *heady stuff*.
Stan:	Ya, a God complex. One factor was always involved— I had to have a drink. Then I totally believed in myself.
Dr. Scott:	You had the whole wide world in your hand.
Stan:	I wouldn't even have to take it, just talk a little and they'd give it to me.

The reader will recall that Pete, in a former quote mentioned killing. In one of the therapy sessions, we did a psychodrama (re-enacted) of this episode and it was so *moving* (or tense or *real*) that there was a sudden alteration in consciousness; when he *came back* (returned to his normal level of awareness he asked, "What happened? What did you do?"

I would say that this is an example of *spontaneous* hypnosis or self-hypnosis, or hypnosis brought about by psychodrama. I have an article (1968) on spontaneous hypnosis and have delivered a talk (1971) on psychodrama leading to hypnosis.

Group hypnosis was used occasionally with rather good results.

As an illustration, one member (Jack) related to the group that during hypnosis:

> I saw a hairy ape trying to cross over the horizon to get to the good guy—which I see as a struggle inside of me, trying to change from being an ape, to fit into society. The good guy was pulling and having a struggle with the ape. The *feeling*, was that the good guy was trying to get rid of the ape.

The group was surprised and fascinated by Jack's experience, but other members had different reactions; for instance:

Jerry:	I kept hearing the cars.
Bob:	Fine—I felt relaxed and at ease. It was good.
Bernie:	Okay—I'll go for it.
Dennis:	I started to relax and then I felt the pressure—pressure, like I felt when going on work-release—so I said, to hell with it. I want none of it.
Jack:	I see you as scared—inside. I've watched you at the Center; if you can get by with joking, you're okay. You're living in a bowl of snakes.
Bernie:	I'm upset—I can't handle things—so I have to have my defenses up.

The dynamic material emerging from the group hypnosis was utilized in following sessions.

During the middle phase, discussions often centered around the causes of crime—or more particularly, the reason for each individual's criminal activity.

I will present illustrations from both groups concerning crime or antisocial behavior, what it meant, how it felt, how it had helped, and eventually how to stop it.

Don:	Laws are for the higher class, they want the laws, not the lower class people.
Joe:	Use Ted Kennedy for an example—if that would have been me—I'd be in jail.
Floyd:	Look at his kids—caught with marijuana, but they get off.
Don:	Laws are meant for everyone, but they're not enforced.
Bob:	The cons and the doctors that do get caught—the doctors get out sooner.
Bill:	I've never seen a doctor in the Pen, who spent a lot of time. You *get as much justice as you pay for.*

Dr. Scott:	You guys angry at the higher classes?
Don:	At the judges!
Bill:	Rich men can hire their attorneys; poor men are stuck with whatever attorney he gets.
Sam:	My verdict was guilty.
Dr. Scott:	What if all of you were rich—how would you feel then?
Bill:	I'd change my attitude. If I was a millionaire, I'd want stricter laws.
Bob:	So would I.

This is an example how many convicts think—an inability to abstract a concept; rather they are *concrete* about their *bum beef.*

In numerous group sessions, efforts were made to make them accurate in their reality assessments, since as Maslow (1954) notes this is one characteristic of a healthy personality.

In other discussions, I attempted to get each convict to look at his own motivation for *his* crimes—not the crimes of others, or the condition of society.

Below is a group dialogue on this topic:

Paul:	The big thing about crime is the excitement, outsmarting the biggest organization in the world—the FBI, the State Troopers, and the local police. They're all working against you. You just rob a place and get in the car, and the cops are shooting at you. You're a superhero. Then you lose the cops in the car chase and you say, "I lost the fools." Hell, the cops go into being a cop for the same thing—excitement.
Bill:	Is it greater than sexual excitement?
Paul:	Ya, much better! It's in your mind—*all the time.* It's like a mountain climber. It's a challenge. You plan it all out and it works.
Sam:	Not me—not for excitement.
Paul:	Your heart is pounding.
Sam:	For me, it's to relieve pressure. If I didn't have money and feel equal.
Paul:	If that's the case, how do you explain people with money, who go into crime? It's the excitement.
Sam:	Not me—I did it for the money.
Dr. Scott:	Paul, how you going to give up the excitement?
Paul:	I like art and I've got a girl friend.
Joe:	Sex with her?
Paul:	This might sound strange—no sex with her—she's good.

I like her, but I got another girl friend and I have sex with her. Give up the excitement? Well, I did four years in the joint for $1,100—it's not worth it. So now I'm going to school—I've put too many years in prison.

Dr. Scott:	Let's go around and see how the rest of the group feels about their motive for crime.
Homer:	Money.
Fred:	Money. I developed expensive habits.
Doug:	Money.
George:	Personal reasons (homosexual)
Clark:	Drugs—heroin.

In the other group Harry stated when he broke into a house, he became excited and thrilled, "It's just like Christmas Eve. All those presents." He estimated that he *broke into* over two hundred homes more for the *thrill*, than the need for things. It was a matted of principle (pride) that he did not physically break-in (break down doors, etc.) but rather figure a way to get in, and then he would become excited "like Christmas Eve."

The majority of the other convicts in this group therapy session felt another motive or reason was more important. Many agreed with Mel's explanation:

I felt I couldn't do much, and I didn't start growing until I started to steal. I went from job to job, feeling insecure. I didn't have an education. As I began to steal I became a rounder—that is, I could do all different kinds of stealing. *I knew I could take care of myself.* As I became better known, I was sought after (that's a joke) —both by police and by other guys. Before stealing I didn't have any confidence in myself.

George:	Are you trying to change from a rounder to a square John? Why change?
Mel:	Law of averages. I got what I wanted out of the stealing—self confidence; now, I can make it with square John. (Mel differs from the *average con*—yet he later returned to crime).
George:	I have an antisocial attitude. We compete in a pain and pleasure world. I'm afraid of punishment and I get strokes out of some of the things square John does. I got a sense of confidence out of crime, and now I'm trying to change and develop a sense of confidence—to get things legally.

Others felt they had benefited in unique ways. For example, Dave said:

> I was insecure and paranoid, but I got to working on the weights for two years; and I was 140 pounds when I started and now I'm 212. I can benchpress 400 pounds and do squats with 540 pounds. Also, what helped me, at the Forest Camp, was a guy who I hated at first —he had sodomy with a fourteen year old boy, then strangled him —but he helped me by talking to me. I didn't have no schooling and when I put the weight on, I could kick others around.

Perhaps a comment regarding *excitement* as a causative or prompting motivation in convict behavior might be timely.

I have found other patient populations who mention *excitement* as one of principle motivations for their life-style. For instance, a twenty-five-year-old matron stated taking care of her child "— was okay and satisfactory, but it lacks the excitement of the other life—. I never know what's going to happen—." She was referring to the unpredictable events associated with her husband and his *wild* life style.

This, as well as remarks by numerous other patients, indicate that the *payoff* is so rewarding they do not want to give it up. Said a bit differently, some patients and some convicts are not suffering souls, but excitement prone individuals. Burton (1972) indicates a new diagnostic entry, the manipulative personality. He writes, "A key to the dynamics of the manipulative personality is the exhilaration of putting something over on another person."

A two prong factor is operative in some convicts:

1. A subjective, intrapersonal element which the individual takes pleasure in performing certain arts, I call this excitment.
2. An interpersonal factor, putting something over on someone, Burton terms this manipulative.

When both factors are experienced in an existential, subjective manner, the motivation is strong, dynamic and driving.

In their otherwise excellent book, *The Paranoid*, (1970) Swanson *et al*, fail to mention convicts and their paranoid thinking patterns. My experience tends to strongly suggest an association

—or a relationship between being a convict and a paranoid trait in thinking. The recording dialogues in this chapter tend to support this contention.

Swanson (1970) makes the following statement:

> Yet, it (paranoid thinking) is a sufficiently pervasive characteristic of the individual so that once it is evoked, the tendency is for the paranoid approach to remain, as the principle characteristic of a patient's behavior.

Future research must assess the accuracy of this statement. Is this tendency any different than other problems—depression, phobias, etc.?

The discussion above led to a natural transition from life in prison to life outside. It was generally felt that, "Those square John's are so dull;" but an argument developed—half agreeing and half disagreeing—although all did agree that, "In the Joint talking and dreaming are part of life." The putting of the dream into reality (on work-release) is tough. So when it's tough they like to revert to talking and dreaming, even telling about pulling a caper (stealing). This is one way trouble starts.

Often, it seemed to me, that some of the group sent out double messages about the penitentiary. "It's no damn good," yet, "It's not a bad place to be." The following dialogue is partially suggestive of their attitude:

Frank: Most who commit crime *want to get caught,* not consciously, though I suppose some do it consciously. There's not the pressure in the Joint. In there you don't have to worry about the pressure of society. I suppose it's like alcoholics, who blank out their minds because of pressure.

George: I do things to escape from pressure, but I *didn't* want to go to prison.

Frank: My problem is a bad family life. When you get older, you're not trained for the world. My two brothers started me stealing before the first grade. I got my candy stealing. As I got older, I stole cars. I knew what would happen—but I wanted money and cars.

Sam: When you go to prison, the pressure is off, but in a couple of days you're climbing the walls to get out.

Fred: Ya, but how many will come back: It's comfortable in there.

Bill: It's just an extension of being a kid.

Dick: I could see it. Some play cards and watch TV like it. But when you get older, the Joint becomes horrible. Ya, remember that book recalling the sting of the prison is important. (I had taken portions from the book, Deviant Children Grown up by Robins).

From this dialogue and others it certainly appears that convicts have radically different feelings, thoughts, and motives concerning crime and prison. Some don't mind prison, in fact, seem attracted; while others hate prison but are unable to curb their antisocial behavior and focus on the prison instead of themselves.

The first step in my rehabilitation of the convict is that the convict has to experience the need in a very direct way to stay out of trouble.

Jack: I almost blew my job. I couldn't handle the situation. I got so threatened. The wood began to come out of the machine so fast, I couldn't keep up. I walked off. The Boss told me to simmer down. So I came back. Afterwards I heaved up. (Jack is the same individual who had the hypnotic experience of the good guy and the ape.)

Dr. Scott: What's your stomach saying?

Jack: I felt like I wanted to punch somebody.

Dr. Scott: That's your fists. What about your stomach?

Jack: Oh? My work record isn't too good. So I felt I was going back to the Joint. Once the Joint was security. Now, I've got to find another security. (It's pleasant to report that Jack is out of work-release, and just recently dropped in to tell me he was getting married. He seems to be making a good adjustment.)

Hence, convicts differ regarding the motivation of their crimes, as well as how they feel about prison. For some, crime is an *ego trip,* for some crime is the result of personality factors, for others crime stems from early family life, and for others crime is the end result of poor social conditions. Convicts differ about prison —some see prison as security (a Linus blanket); others hate prison with a passion.

To indulge in broad generalizations either about crime or rehabilitation, is not only unwarranted, but inaccurate. Those who do, indulge in a simplistic, *missing-link* theory.

In the middle phase of group, the members began to recognize an important and rather consistant pattern while on work-release, which consisted of the following:

1. Upon release from prison, they typically experience a kind of *psychological-honeymoon*.
2. This often turned into *reality-confusion* consisting of the following factors:
   a) things don't go well at work
   b) trouble at the center-infrigement of rules
   c) confusion about their future roles—as worker, or husband, etc.
   d) some wish to return to the Joint; others become angry, some seek avoidance,—alcohol, etc.
3. Some were alcoholics and this was troublesome. Alcohol was a constant source of either temptation or trouble. Eventually, an agreement was reached between the alcoholic convict and prison authorities, in which the convict agreed to take Antabuse *before* release from prison, and to continue Antabuse while on work-release. Elsewhere, I (1970) have written on alcoholics and treatment, and that work can be consulted by the interested reader.
4. Gradually, a *shaping-up*, and adjustment appears.

It is especially helpful to have a group member in phase 4 help a group member in phase 2.

FINAL PHASE

The final phase approached when the inmate is nearing his parole date. From a point of view of time, this differed—that is; one inmate in group might just be starting on work release and another nearing his hearing before the Parole Board.

As each member's time got *short* (approached the time for his hearing) he was given a little extra time in the group to express his anxieties and his problems. Perhaps Dan's summary is somewhat typical, "When the time get shorter, it get's tougher. I'm getting tense facing the free world. I've been locked up a long time." While Hal said it a little differently, "I'm feeling funny. I have to take care of myself. It feels good, but also scary."

In this final phase certain modalities and themes were developed. I will discuss some of the more prevalent ones.

1. Some of the group suggested that one of the men on work-release return to the Joint (prison) and talk to the men who were to be placed on work-release, since the prevalent information was from the ones *busted*, who didn't make it. They were, as a rule bitter and attempted to give the work-release program a *bad name*.

2. When I gave a presentation to the Department of Psychiatry at the University of Oregon Medical School on therapy for convicts, Harry and Mel participated. They made an excellent addition to to my talk.

3. Some of the members were requested by the Parole Board to attend the group therapy sessions after release—for a time. This appears to be an effective follow-through.

4. Discussion often revolved around, "Can convicts change?" The following group dialogue will give a *flavor* to this topic.

George: Not all the guys in the Joint are convicts, an habitual criminal is a convict.

Dr. Scott: Are you a convict, John?

John: I guess I am.

Ken: A *convict* is solid, an *inmate isn't* — an inmate isn't as strong or as hard.

Dr. Scott: Some first timers could be.

Ken: Ya, could be.

Dr. Scott: Are you Clark?

Clark: I'm one—I'm a five time loser—so I've experienced more than an inmate.

Dr. Scott: Inmates can change, but not convicts?

Leo: Any man can change.

Ken: No.

All the Group: That's not right.

Dr. Scott: It's *easier* to change inmates.

John: An inmate is a first timer—he isn't used to it. Once it's a habit, it's hard to change.

Sam: I've never thought like a convict—I'm square. I never associated with 'em in the Joint. I just did my time.

Ed: I know if something good turned up—I'd steal it—I'd have to.

Willie: He's a convict—he wants *money!*

Ed: I just got mad—all kinds of deductions, so last year before going to the Joint, I started to steal.

John: You're kidding yourself—I don't like to pay taxes—but I have to. My girl friend is waiting for me—she's my fall partner—she drove the car.

Dr. Scott: You'll return to the Joint.

John: No, too much time—five years is enough. I felt that in the Joint—that the Joint made me bitter—*It was my own thinking.* The first night in Jail was the best night's sleep in years. I didn't like what I was doing—I wanted to quit, but I didn't, I had to keep going. When I was caught—it might sound stupid, I was feeling sorry for myself, my wife had left me, God, the way I pulled some jobs—I wanted to be shot.

Dr. Scott: Your girl friend—no influence? Just a fall partner?

John: She asked me to stop pulling the jobs, but I didn't care, I didn't care for anything—I was just killing time.

Pat: I'm not a convict—I don't think like one. Hard core convicts—all they're interested in, is the big *I*. A convict would spend five dollars to beat you out of five cents.

Sam: At one time I was out to beat everyone.

Pat: During the day, the convict is a big wheeler, at night—he's lonely, some cry.

Dan: At night, we get to feeling sorry for ourselves.

Pat: A convict tries to hide his emotions, at night he lets go of 'em.

John: Are you more content at night?

Pat: I'm *home* now, you know. (Pat is referring to his release—but he still comes.) We moved yesterday, so last night the wife and kids went for a drive and got some ice cream. We then drove to the center and I couldn't go in eating on an ice cream cone! I had my wife hold it.

Dan: You had to keep your image up.

Dr. Scott: You had to suddenly change from Daddy—to a man!

Pat: Ya, gosh—is that it? Wow! I had to drop being Daddy and be a man!

Joe: What's wrong with eating ice cream?

John: A kid?

Pat: I had to be a man.

5. Another topic was that of making choices—the ability to choose and not to blame one's choices on others or to believe that one can't choose. The following is a group dialogue on choices.

Dr. Scott: What about your *choices?*

Bill: I hated you, Sam—cause you had *inside* you, rebellion, that I couldn't get.

Sam: I choose what I want.

Bill: In the cell, after the doors were closed, I could relax. When the doors opened—I put on a front.

Sam: I never said, I'm no good. I fought them in the Joint—but I realized I had to make choices.

Bill: I'm different. I had only a third grade education and I was ashamed of it. Lt. Jones helped me with math and reading, so I began to feel an obligation to him. The riot came and Lt. Jones was hurt; and I told him, "If they get you, they got to get me," and then the group said, "We want *all* those Bulls." I found I was a coward. I put a blanket over Lt. Jones and ran to the yard. I got wiped out. After the riot, when I saw him I couldn't face him. Up to that time, I didn't think I was afraid. *Now*, I'd stay with him. It came as a surprise, I thought of myself as brave—lots of guts.

Dr. Scott: Guts—but no backbone.

Sam: I like that—but me, if I felt obligated, I'd stay. Damn—here's that conscious.

Bill: I had to sneak out—no one saw it—but I did.

Robert: I'm a coward too, but when I'm drunk, I'm brave. All my life I've blamed others. Bill, you came out with something good—that bit, about pleasing others. I'd keep everything in—except the anger. Sam, you, I always thought you were a hard nose—two years ago I wouldn't be in the same room with you.

Group therapy can further *push-along*, or combine what other therapeutic modalities set in motion—for instance a healing experience, or altered state of consciousness or conversion.

Ludwig (1970) spells out what he considers to be the essential element of a true or real, or lasting *healing experience*. Ludwig's remarks are concerned with professional therapeutic techniques.

The following, is an account by one of the members in the group, Art. It is my opinion that it is a true or real *healing experience*.

a) there was an altered state of consciousness,
b) a feeling of *rebirth* or renaissance followed,
a) there was an altered state of consciousness,
   lasted for four years. (See Appendix 3).

During one of the sessions, a newspaper reporter was present and later an article appeared. After the article, I asked Pete how he felt—since his correct name was used.

Dr. Scott: When you saw that article in the Oregonian, what did you think?

Pete: I wasn't ashamed of what I said—but I thought of those reading it at the Joint! There goes my image! I'm be-

ginning to laugh. Hm! In the Pen, I had a deep hatred
—I've changed. Wait! I could fool people, but *there is a change*. So God, I didn't realize it, in a way, in the writing—here in group, yes, but there it was *in writing*. I had to admit to myself, then I got to thinking, what would happen if they put me back in the Joint, in my imagination—a situation, like that—I'm not so sure. (See Appendix 4).

Joe: What about the outside? That's more important—if you make it out here, you won't have to go back.

Pete: I'm making it. But it's tough. In the Joint I was running on *hate, it was easy*. Now, it's tough. I'm trying to meet 'em, Dr. Scott, Gordon—they're trusting me. I used to hate the Bulls.

Dr. Scott: The more you like yourself, the less you hate others.

Pete: WOW! Ya!

A fairly recent (six months) innovation is to have the women on work-release join the group of men. My estimation, as well as the group members, is that this adds to the group's meaningfulness and practicality. To mention, but one among several useful factors, role playing between *husband and wife* can now become more real as a result.

In the early section of this chapter I presented some therapeutic *stances*, I had taken. Now, I would want to add to those opening remarks and reflect on the type or *kind* of therapy employed during the 3½ year period.

Initially, the group members were allowed to ventilate. This could be termed supportive therapy. Later in the sessions, suggestive (hypnotic) and insightful techniques were periodically employed. Timing is essential.

The principle therapeutic modality utilized could be termed *thought therapy*, which is comprised of the following major characteristics.

1. How one thinks is critically important in determining one's behavior. If, for instance, "Odds don't mean anything," behavior based on that thinking will ensue.
2. Make the individual think about *how* he thinks.
3. It's the individual's responsibility to change from being a *bad chooser* to a *good chooser*. No excuses, rationalizations, *bum beef*, or *B.S.* will be tolerated—that's kid stuff.

4. There are some thoughts and feelings which the convict can't afford to *indulge* in.
5. In order to assist the convict in this particular kind of therapy, the therapist can:
   a) point out the convict's poor thought processes
   b) challenge his major assumptions
   c) present new things to think about
   d) model good thought processes himself
   e) try to be a man—at all times; good techniques *performed* by a *whimp* don't get air-borne.

RESULTS

What about results? Results, in this area are difficult to assess— but an assessment is mandatory.

It is my clinical impression that several—perhaps many, even most of the men who attended group therapy benefited, at least to some degree.

A few, perhaps some, were substantially helped in their emotional growth and thought processes. I feel there are *clinical facts* which substantiate this opinion—a few of which I have presented above.

For more *objective facts*—records which indicate what happened on an overt level and some of the realistic developments flowing from the group, the reader can refer to Chapter X.

From an experiential point of view—as a group therapist — I found it more personally demanding than other groups, but also more rewarding.

REFERENCES

1. Abrahamson, D.: *The Psychology of Crime.* Columbia University, New York, 1960.
2. Beck, A.: *Depression.* Hoeber Medical Division, Harper and Row, New York, 1970.
3. Burton, B.: The manipulative personality. *Archives of General Psychiatry, 26*:318-321, 1972.
4. Clark, R.: *Crime in America.* Simon and Schuster, New York, 1970.
5. Ludwig, A., Levine, J., and Stark, L.: *LSD and Alcoholism.* Thomas, Springfield, 1970.
6. MacLean, P.: Man and his animal brains. *Modern Medicine,* Feb., pp. 95-106, 1964.
7. Maslow, A.: *Motivation and Personality.* Harper and Row, New York, 1954.

8. Robins, Lee: *Deviant Children Grown Up.* Williams and Wilkins Co., Baltimore, 1966.
9. Scott, E.: Hypnosis without conscious intent in an alcoholic. *Quarterly Journal of Studies on Alcohol,* 29:709-711, 1968.
10. Scott, E.: *Struggles in an Alcoholic Family.* Thomas, Springfield, 1970.
11. Scott, E.: Talk and unpublished lecture given at Grand Rounds, Department of Psychiatry, University of Oregon Medical School, 1971.
12. Skinner, B.: *Beyond Freedom and Dignity.* Alfred A. Knopf, New York, 1971.
13. Swanson, D., Bohert, P., and Smith, J.: *The Paranoid.* Little, Brown and Co., Boston, 1970.

APPENDIX 1

A Group Member's Account of Group Therapy and Thinking

Perhaps life should be one long therapy session.

Seven months ago I would hardly have expected to say this, let alone believe it, but the change I have experienced in my life is sufficient enough proof that it is a valid statement. Seven months ago I was released from prison. I came out of prison with essentially the same set of problems with which I entered; I was alcoholic; frustrated by an active guilt complex; and plagued by feelings of shame and inadequacy.

As a provision of my parole I was required to attend group therapy. For about the first two months, there was relatively little change in either my situation or my attitude; namely, that I didn't have any problems. It was at about this time that I became aware of an idea that was entirely new to me. How was I thinking? At first it was not an easy question to answer. Mainly because my attitude, or way of thinking was standing in the way of the answer. However, the thought provoking nature of the question and seeing how other people in my therapy group were dealing with the question finally enabled me to find an answer.

How was I thinking?

I was thinking of the easiest way out of my parole without actually having to become involved in any way. In other words, playing a totally dishonest game with, not only myself, but with the rest of my therapy group, my loved ones and friends and perhaps the whole world.

This brought about a rude awakening. I began to look at myself in terms of honesty, integrity, loyalty. These were not new words to me; but they were new ideas that invoked new and uncomfortable feelings within me.

It was then that my life really began to change. I had to accept loyalty and realize to whom I felt loyal. To maintain this sense of loyalty, I had to be honest; and being honest I began to feel a degree of integrity and self respect I had not known previously in my life.

My life has not changed completely. I still have problems,

168

worries and trials. But, my attitude toward these things and toward others and myself has changed.

I am married now and the woman to whom I am married feels these same things that I do. We talk a great deal about our inner selves. We reveal to each other what goes on inside ourselves, both the good and the bad, and by so doing, we minimize the pressures which result from holding things inside and we make each day of loyalty, honesty, and self respect so much easier to realize.

This is what I mean when I say that perhaps all of life should be a group therapy session. If a person can learn to be honest, even with just one another, it is a beginning.

APPENDIX 2

Group Discussion

Bob:	The death penalty is cruel—sitting and waiting for the chamber! Most crimes are in passion, others like—he's sick.
Sue:	I was glad when it was abolished. I was a victim of circumstances.
Dr. Scott:	How would you feel, wating for the gas chamber?
Sue:	I'd want them to do it right away. Waiting would blow my mind.
Dr. Scott:	Would you have gone crazy?
Sue:	I probably would have. I was really emotional when I did it. (*It* refers to the murder she committed).
Jack:	If I was facing it, I'd rather they'd gas me, than twenty years.
Hue:	I'd be better off gassed, than confine me for years.
Bob:	I'm not sure about what you guys are saying. Human nature has a need to survive.
Jack:	Not for me, no way.
Bob:	Next Saturday you're going to be gassed—or twenty years!
Jack:	I'd walk in the gas chamber.
Dan:	I used to think that way, but I've sure changed. There's always something to look forward to.
Jack:	I've done hard time—I used to laugh at it, when I was younger.
Bob:	One keeps hoping.
Betty:	No right to take your life. (She was in jail for killing someone by a car accident).

Jake: No justice—in an eye for an eye. (He had hit someone over the head—in his robbery.)

Sue: I've punished myself. I think of how it could have been avoided.

Dr. Scott: Do you dream of him?

Sue: Ya, but he's living in my dreams.

Paul: I'm glad they abolished capital punishment, but not for all cases—not for murder of children.

Sam: I'm glad capital punishment is abolished because the rich man never gets it—just the poor.

Fred: I can't see mass murder. I think someone like that, who kills a lot of people, should be hung.

Nina: Taking a life is never justified—those mass killers are mentally ill.

Pete: Some people can't be helped. They've chosen a way of life, and it's not wrong to them. I used to do a lot of gaming.

Paul: Some crimes are so cruel—the way of killing. In the prison, I heard a guy, while holding a pistol to the victim's head, ask him, "How do you think it will feel to die?" and as the guy is talking, shoots him. A guy like that deserves capital punishment.

Sam: Or the cold murderer—who can be hired to wipe out a guy—he's not in a heat of passion, or mentally ill.

APPENDIX 3
Art's Story

About four years ago, I found myself lying in the drunk tank of the city jail, facing numerous charges, including armed robbery. Being a three time loser, I knew what was in store, a life sentence in the State Penitentiary. There would be no way out for many, many years to come. At this time I could see nothing ahead but a vast darkness which left me in a state of mind contemplating ways in which I could destroy myself. I was lost and lonely and felt no love in life which left nothing but ending it all.

How I ended up in such a situation was built upon my past thirty years of life. As a child I was very sensitive, wanting love and attention. However, circumstances prevented family relations from being one of love. My stepfather, being an alcoholic and my mother working all the time left no alternative other than for us kids to live places other than at home. I was moved from children's home to foster homes to relatives homes which left me very hurt. I was hurt because I felt my mother didn't love me and because she didn't, I was sure no one else did either. Even though I felt unwanted, I still searched for love. The first few homes I encountered I tried to join in with the rest of the group, but was pushed aside because I wasn't part of the family. I would withdraw, going somewhere by myself, making out my own worlds and friends.

I didn't feel very worthwhile but I still wanted friendship and love. During my first year in school I ran across a jar of money in the classroom. I stole the money and brought some of the other children things which gained me acceptance with them. For the first time in my life I felt as if I had real friends and I learned that I had to give something other than myself to gain friends. It really felt good to have the other kids like me.

My buying of love progressed on through the years. I wrote checks, committed burglaries and robbed stores and banks in order to gain money for my worth. Being the lost and lonely person that I was, I was actually living in the only real world I knew. However, deep inside I knew that the whole situation was phoney. To escape from the thoughts that people didn't like me at all, only what I could give them, I turned to narcotics for relief. During periods of time when I had no money or narcotics, I would walk the streets for hours and days at a time, thinking that someone would reach out in real friendship. This never happened, so I just went on until I could make my next score. This is why I could see nothing ahead but darkness.

When reaching the penitentiary for the fourth time with a life sentence, my thoughts were still on how to end it all. However, I couldn't bring myself to the point of doing it because of the hate for the man involved in my last crime spree. He gained his freedom for his testimony against me, which left me with a bitter hatred for him. For this reason, I could see living so that I could one day get outside the walls to get even wtih him. For periods of time I would just lay in my cell just planning how to kill him. After doing three or four months of my life sentence, a friend sent me a birthday present asking me if I would read it. This birthday present happened to be a Bible. I was very reluctant to read it as I had never read the Bible before.

I promised I would, so I started reading. In the very first few pages I knew that what was being said was the complete truth. I found myself doing nothing but searching the scriptures, looking for answers. What I found was that God loved me more than anything else in the world. Wanting to gain a closeness with Him and the love He offers, I honestly and sincerely opened my heart, confessing that I was lost and asked for the new life He promised. As His word says, "If we confess our sins, He is faithful and Just to forgive us our sins and cleanse us from all unrighteousness." Something happened in those moments that I still can't fully explain except to say that I had personal experience with the Living God. A great weight of burdens and guilts lifted off me and I felt light as a feather, almost as if I could float off the bed. The sensation that I had go through me, is too beautiful for words. I wanted nothing else to do with the world or anything in it, and I asked God to be with Him. I fell into the most peaceful sleep that I have ever had in my entire life.

The next morning I got out of bed feeling like a new person. I was truthfully happy and felt a real love for the first time in my life. My whole attitude about life was changed and I could see a bright, wonderful future. As the Scripture says, "If any man be in Christ, he is a new creation, old things have passed away and all things become new." This is exactly the way it was. I felt like a brand new person. I was alive for the very first time. For about thirty days after my experience, I went through the penitentiary holding Sunday School seven days a week. I wanted to tell everyone what Christ had done for me. Some thought I had flipped my cookie because I was running around with a big smile on my face. One guy even told me that I shouldn't be happy because I was doing life. I was on a high that in no way compares with any dope I've ever taken. I felt wonderful and I didn't have to take a pill or stick a needle in my arm to feel that way. But it wasn't long until I found myself confronted with my old hangups and problems of loneliness, rejection and lack of communication with others. But I found I had strength within me to face problems and want to overcome them. I entered into group therapy through the prison program. It took me a period of time before I was able to relate to other members of the group because of a fear of rejection and a lack of self-worth. I didn't want to talk but I forced myself to do so and the first few times of speaking out was a shaking experience which left me trembling all over with fright. After a period of time, I found acceptance no matter what I said and I gained confidence. I was then able to contribute to the group by just being myself. I found that we all have problems that seem like monsters but are actually small, little items once we bring them out. I am now able to communicate with any and everybody because I feel worthwhile and have a contribution by just being a living whole person. I have found a real like for people and this has been gained through therapy sessions. I am now out of prison after only serving 3½ years. I am now working as a counselor with men who are in prison. The full success of the past three years I fully accredit to God. God gave me a new life and directed my growth. And group therapy has been a tremendous part of my growth with Christ.

When I presented a lecture to five hundred university students, on drug abuse and avenues of help, Art was helpful and effective —making a good impression on the students. He is now employed as an aide in a state operated drug program doing a very satisfactory job.

APPENDIX 4

A Letter from Pete

Pete was returned to prison for a relatively minor violation. During his stay he wrote the following letter.

Dear Dr. Scott.

I could feel lost and sad and troubled and anxious and guilty and bewildered. I could feel like nothing, absolutely nothing. I could consider suicide, even wish for it. I could feel hate in my heart. I feel love, but OK, how easy it could be for me to believe that love made matters worse rather than better. I could exaggerate the extreme fears and tearing uncertainties that are at this moment pressing in on me. But to do so Dr. Scott would make you a failure and me nothing.

The crushing thought that I have failed attacks me unmercifully. It is awfully hard to face the terrible fact that I have failed. Failed you, failed myself, failed Betty. But the more I think about failing I realize that I have not failed. More important, Dr. Scott, my beloved friend, you have not failed. Please believe that. If you could feel and know what is in my heart at this moment, as I lay on this bunk, in this cell, waiting to be returned to the one place in my life that has brought fear, horror, despair, anguish, AND HATE. You would know that you were not a failure. Where anger and fear and hate have been, there is now love and understanding. It is the most delightful and beautiful feeling I have ever experienced. I tingle and became dizzy with delight to know that *I* could continue to function in spite of the deep disturbances and interior terrors that were overwhelming me. I actually tried to hate to protect myself from that I thought was coming. I failed again. I can't even succeed in getting mad and hating. I guess I'm doomed to be a failure.

Would you believe what pleased me about myself was I did not wish to blame others, and above all, myself with self-pity, for my failure to make it on parole. Instead I have an overwhelming desire to comprehend, reevaluate, and reweight my experiences after searching my mind and soul about my problems. I want to reach a point where I can view my problems from a better perspective. But in order to do this I have to relive many moments of my life, no matter how painful they have been to me. By trying to understand my problems I am beginning to understand myself. I am learning who I am and what I am. See, my dear friend, you have not failed, I have not failed, because I am going back to prison. What we started out to discover about me —we have. Many people have failed and made good later. More important, what you have taught me to see is that some of us have to fail in order to succeed. There are very seldom successes without some failures along the way, and if there are, it is for the exceptionally fortunate of this world. I can't go on failing indefinitely in life, but in view of the different new doors that have been open to me, I can allow myself some degree of failure without feeling that my life as a whole has been a failure.

When the two detectives flashed their badges and placed me

under arrest, by order of the Parole Board, a sickening and chilling feeling spread over my entire body, and my mind seemed to freeze, even cease to exist. In a daze I asked if I could see the warrant. They were quite kind and even apologetic. As I read the warrant the words that jerked me back to what really was happening to me were, "He is hot tempered and should be considered extremely dangerous." That is the moment I thought of you Dr. Scott and all that we have accomplished in the sixteen months we have known each other. For a moment I almost succumbed to the frightening thought that all our talks, all our searching does not make any difference to the Parole Board. To them I am hot tempered and extremely dangerous. Since they knew that about me, I was going to believe them infallible, and act exactly as they knew me to be. But you know what, I failed again. I could not become a raven, dangerous, savage Indian. I guess they know something about me I don't know and I'll have to ask them what it is. Even the detectives thought it strange and amusing. Apologized, shook their heads and wished me luck.

Dr. Scott please don't be disappointed in me. Because I have changed, even if the Parole Board does not think I have. Because of you Dr. Scott I do not have that terrible sense of loneliness, abandonment, and betrayal. You have taught me not to bury my feelings and bottle up my emotions. Because of you I have ceased to strive desperately to become someone I thought that I had to become. That is no longer important to me. Instead I have come to believe that the most important thing is to succeed in my relationship with other people. I want to reach out to other people now. I don't identify with everyone and everything bad and awful anymore. You have made me feel valuable and loved and have helped me to be strong enough to stand on my own two feet and to feel that I am worth something. I no longer feel lost and without meaning, and I am somebody, not just number ————.

In my effort to understand my problems, I have come to know more about myself that I might have otherwise. I am no longer stumbling around blindly, and I think I shall have a better perspective of what is important and what is not, and I shall keep the unimportant out of the important part of my life. I think I shall be a better person in spite of my going back to prison. I know myself better, and perhaps someday I can leave prison, never to return. I know my faults, but I accept them now. I feel the pain of the realization that I am not without weakness, but these I accept as well. I hope I shall not be afraid as I have been. I hope there will be less need of my protective shell. I must forget the past and look to my new-found future. I do not think that one must reject one's past completely, no matter if it consists of failures. If you reject it, you draw nothing from it. You cannot redeem your past, but you can use it to go forward.

Maybe some wonderful day I won't need any help. This, above all, is our goal, doctor. I like to believe there is always hope. I feel I am now better equipped to withstand whatever is in store for me without breaking. From here on in I shall put every experience in life to good use no matter how useless and painful it seems.

You, then my lovely and wonderful Betty have given me keys to all kinds of new doors that I knew were there all along, but I couldn't find the keys to unlock them. I continue to need a helping hand, and right now that hand comes from my Betty's. She writes and visits when she can. You got me to my feet—now she helps me walk. The time will come, unforced and unbidden, when I shall need no help. I must love her enough to believe that these fears will pass and that they will not be with me forver. I must, above all, believe that it need not be the end, as I once thought it had to be, if I ever went back to prison.

I guess all this means Dr. Scott is sixteen months ago you started me down a road, I was unfamiliar with, and even feared. Then Betty came along and helped me find the real me. She has made me feel that I can go anywhere in the world and be accepted. She has shown me that everywhere in the world there are people like me, and I no longer have to feel like an outsider all alone. Because she stands beside me and loves me. Together you both have made me feel like a human being loved, wanted, cared about, but more important, a human being now capable of love, caring and wanting another being. I will do everything to solve my problems, because I want to more than anything else in the world, and I will, but the place I am going to sure isn't the ideal place to solve problems. Learning is an endless process, and sometimes a painful one.

Pray for me Dr. Scott, and don't forget me, please! I shall never forget you. As a matter of fact I shall never forget all of the group. They all helped me and I love them all. Give them my regards and tell them like General MacArthur, I shall return. That I shall not fail to do.

Until we meet again, I am respectfully—Oh! Baloney! With all my love, your greatful friend,

He was not held in prison long (one month), is now employed and his employer states that he is an excellent employee.

CHAPTER XII

POLICE AND THE MENTAL HEALTH PROFESSIONAL: A CASE OF DESERTION

EDWARD M. COLBACH

AND

CHARLES D. FOSTERLING

THIS CHAPTER WILL explore the role of the police officer as a mental health care-giver and the relationship between the police officer and the mental health professional. The paper consists of the following four parts: (1) an explanation of who we, the authors, are; (2) a discussion of the title idea; (3) a discussion of police culture and the helping process; and (4) a summary and some conclusions.

WHO WE ARE

To place in proper perspective the observations made in this chapter, it is necessary to describe who we are in some detail. For the past seventeen months, we, a psychiatrist and a psychiatric social worker, have spent most of our professional time working with law enforcement personnel in the Portland, Oregon, metropolitan area. We have functioned as teachers, consultants, and especially students. Our experience has been limited in time but very intense. A formal description of our program, officially called the Family Crisis Project, is as follows.

General Perspective

The police officer is a significant mental health care-giver. Wilson (1968) has pointed out that only 10 percent of police calls are strictly law enforcement in nature. The others fall into the categories of information gathering, services and order maintenance. Bard (1970) has done pioneering work in New York in training special teams of officers to respond to family disturbances.

A survey of almost four hundred local officers in Portland, Oregon (1967) indicated that they strongly wanted more training in the area of human behavior. The only formal training in human behavior provided by the local departments has consisted of lectured material for recruits at the Metropolitan Police Academy.

Aware of the above the Multnomah County, Oregon, Sheriff's Department in 1969 sought federal money through the Law Enforcement Assistance Administration to establish an applied training program in human behavior. The Sheriff's Department is a very progressive agency, having a four-year college degree requirement for new officers. (Portland is in Multnomah County, but the larger Portland Police Bureau is a separate entity from the Sheriff's Department of about two hundred officers). Grant money was obtained in 1970 for a training project similar to Bard's, under the auspices of the Columbia Region Association of Governments (CRAG). A stipulation of the grant was that training be available on a regional basis to all four of the counties that CRAG serves. This includes more than twenty different law enforcement agencies.

By the time the money became available, the Sheriff who had initiated the idea had been replaced, and his successor was at first cautious about becoming involved in new training projects. Many of the other police agencies in the area were either disinterested or hostile to the idea. They equated the project with trying to make police officers into *social workers,* a distasteful concept.

Staff for the Project was available and eager—it consisted of a 90% time Board-certified psychiatrist as Director, and a full time psychiatric social worker as Coordinator. The Director recently had completed a stint in the U.S. Army, with service in Vietnam, and he wanted to pursue further some of the principles of communiy psychiatry he had learned in the military. The Coordinator had left his clinical job after many years to return to school for a Masters degree in Public Health, and he too was eager to do some challenging community work. Aware of the need but very discouraged by the resistance on the part of the police command presonnel, the staff decided to give it a try. Officially the Project began in October of 1970. There was certainly complete freedom regarding activities, a by-product of the disinterest. The hostility was hard to take.

The Sheriff of Multnomah County opened the door for a five day training session in *Understanding People* for sixteen police recruits in December of 1970. The recruits received the session so well that another session was requested for experienced officers, and the Project was *off and running*.

The Project is still struggling. At this time, however, the Project is engaged in a variety of training and consultation activities, and is providing some direct after-hours emergency services in support of the Multnomah County Sheriff's Department. In this area there are virtually no formal after-hours mental health services available, outside of the County Hospital Psychiatric Ward.

The very survival of this Project for seventeen months is an achievement. But its death is not imminent. The Project has a reservoir of good will established at this time, and it is being asked to join the Multnomah County Mental Health Clinic. This is a very traditional agency with little activity outside its walls. The current plan is for this Project to become the Law Enforcement Program of that agency as of April 1, 1972. This will assure the continued existence of the Project and will help that agency to make a desired change in its philosophy and its amount of extramural activity.

Actual details of the program are as follows.

Purpose of Project

The purpose of this Project is to create a formal meeting ground between police officers and clinicians in the behavioral sciences so that interpersonal problems encountered by police can be handled in the most effective way.

Scope of Project

At this time the Project has these two main objectives: (1) to provide training and consultation in human behavior to police officers and agencies in the CRAG jurisdiction (Multnomah, Washington, Clackamas, and Columbia counties); (2) to provide some emergency mental health services to the population served by the Multnomah County Sheriff's Department in conjunction with that Department.

Methods

To reach the stated objectives, the Project staff engages in the following activities:

(1) For purposes of training and consultation:

(a) Regional, five day training seminars are conducted on a monthly basis. These seminars in *Understanding People* are each attended by twelve to fourteen officers. These personalized seminars include interviews with actual patients at the Psychiatric Crisis Unit of the Multnomah County Hospital and at the Multnomah County Mental Health Clinic; role playing with videotape feedback; meetings with blacks, *longhairs,* and other groups antagonistic toward police; lectures; small group meetings; and sensitivity exercises. Fourteen such seminars have been held.

(b) A course in applied psychology, including many of the techniques mentioned above in (a), is regularly taught in the Portland Community College Department of Public Safety. The third such course has been completed recently. These courses are usually limited to twelve officers.

(c) The staff participates in the training of recruits at the Metropolitan Police Academy, again using many of the techniques mentioned in (a). During the last academy session, the staff had almost three weeks of teaching duties, which included two evenings of group meetings with the recruits and their wives.

(d) The staff participates in other area training activities as the need arises and time permits. (For example, the staff was in charge of the Law Enforcement Section at the five day Western Institute of Drug Problems held in Portland in August of 1971).

(e) The staff is available for consultation to local police agencies upon request. This has been, to date, an under-utilized service.

(2) For purposes of providing emergency mental health services in conjunction with the Multnomah County Sheriff's Department:

(a) The staff provides on-call (available by phone and in person if necessary) supervision for the after-hours field placement of three graduate social work students from Portland State University. The goal is to provide service when most other agencies are unavailable. Since October, 1971, each of these students has spent one night a week riding in a Multnomah County Sheriff's patrol car, teamed with a regular officer. This *counseling team* is used to respond to particular interpersonal crisis which are called to the attention of the Sheriff's Department. The staff also provides individual supervison for these students, and group supervision for all members of the teams.

(b) In the near future the Project will hire another psychiatric social worker who will have an office in patrol headquarters and will expand the services mentioned in (a). He will also do follow-up visits on police contacts.

(c) The staff spends about a total of eight hours per week riding in patrol cars to help implement (a) above and to gather material for training, as well as to be on hand for informal consultation. This is usually after-hours.

(d) The staff is constantly alert for problems in the delivery of mental health services in support of officers, and attempting to correct them. For example, the staff has helped set up a number of meetings between police officers and the personnel of the Multnomah County Hospital Psychiatric Crisis Unit, to smooth out problems between the police and that unit.

Staffing of Project

The Project staff consists of a 90 percent time psychiatrist as Director, a full time psychiatric social worker as Coordinator, and a part time secretary. Numerous other individuals are hired as needed to perform specific functions.

Funding

The Project is funded by the Federal Law Enforcement Assistance Administration under the auspices of the Omnibus Crime Control Act of 1968. Current fiscal year budget is $64,000. A budget for fiscal year 1972 (July) of $57,000 is assured. The OLEC Grant number is 70A 137-2.3.

Evaluation

Upon completing the forty hour seminars, each officer is asked to evaluate it. The first question reads: "Was this seminar worth the time spent?" Only two participants so far did not think it was.

A more formal evaluation of the forty hour seminars was recently done by Milton K. Davis, Ph.D., of Northwest Psychological Services, Portland. He supervised 125 home interviews of people who had recently called the Multnomah County Sheriff's Department for help during interpersonal crisis. Sixty-two interviews of people concerned officers who had the training and sixty-three who had not had it. There was no measurable significant difference between the two groups in their handling of crisis calls, as viewed by the citizenry.

The evaluation however produced some important by-products. The general response of the citizenry was so positive to the police that the police are quite favorable in allowing such studies. The warm response to the interviewer, and the safety he always felt, were important factors in police approval of the plan to hire a full time social worker to work with them and make follow-up visits. The nonthreatened, objective response of the staff to the fact that their training had no measurable effect served to increase their credibility. As a result of the evaluation, some changes in the training are contemplated.

Addendum

Flexibility and inventiveness remain the hallmark of this project. Therefore it is impossible to predict the future project activities with much accuracy, since the project will change as the needs and opportunities change. For example, it is anticipated that this summer one or two medical students from the University of Oregon Medical School will be assigned to the project, and some meaningful experience will be provided for them. A medical student worked with the project last summer, and studied child abuse. A hope is that eventually a small cadre of officers in each of the major departments will receive continuing training so that they can function as true mental health paraprofessionals.

A Case of Desertion

Based on the experiences we described in the lengthy introduction of ourselves, we hardly think we can qualify as experts on police. If anything these past months have taught us how necessary it is to cast aside the expert role and to become students again. Too often the contacts of other professional with the police means the *expert's* lecture. This is often given with the best of intentions but with the least of practical knowledge of where the officers are and what they face on the street. Officers have been somewhat conditioned to sit back, listen cynically, and discount it all as impractical. They do live in a somewhat different world than many of us, and only with a real understanding of this world can we be of help to them. Our patrol car riding has brought this point home more strongly than anything else we have done, and we think that anyone who would work effectively with the police has to spend some time in this activity.

Having disclaimed the expert role, we would like to devote the rest of this chapter to passing on some of our observations to mental health professionals and to those in other disciplines who are interested in helping the police serve the public better. Primarily we are speaking to mental health professions, since this is what we are, and this is the field we know best. We certainly do not claim any infallibility for our observations, and admit that they are open to debate.

It is our contention that the police officer is a significant mental health care giver, serving primarily those people who express their difficulties in acts and in disordered life styles, and who seldom establish significant contact with those formal agencies designed to help people with emotional problems. Mazer (1972) has included in these *parapsychiatric events* such things as fines, probation, jail sentences, juvenile delinquency, marital dissolution, premarital pregnancy, some automobile accidents, auto license withdrawal, alcohol problems, and suicide attempts and suicide.

It is a further contention that in his struggles to deal effectively with problems such as those mentioned, the police officer has largely been deserted by mental health professionals.

This desertion takes a number of forms. First, is the fact that there has often been little or no communication between police and mental health professionals. Second, there has been a pattern for most mental health agencies to be open only during *normal weekday working hours*. As any officer will tell you, this is when the least is happening. Further, there has been the unwillingness of many agencies to reach out beyond their walls to those so-called *unmotivated* people who will not come to the agency. And then, perhaps worst of all, there has been the tendency of some mental health professionals to decry *poor police handling of this situation* without any concept of what it is like to be a policeman on the street.

Before looking at some of the possible reasons for this desertion, we would like to explain the problem in more detail.

In this locale, which we do not think is atypical, most of the formal mental health agencies are only open during regular working hours. There is a psychiatric ward at the County Hospital which provides around-the-clock service for some seriously disturbed *(danger to self or others)* people. Beyond this one facility, there is no service of any magnitude available. There are a few agencies trying to provide some after-hours service, especially for young people, but these are quite limited.

This means that the police officer is the only one really available for twenty-four hour, seven day a week service, including house calls, for a wide variety of emotionally disturbed people.

Things do happen after-hours. Police officers, especially younger ones, are very action-oriented people. In our training seminars it is hard for many of them to sit still. For this reason we try to teach by action (e.g., role playing). The younger officers, wanting *to be where the action is,* always prefer the *swing* shift (4:00 p.m. to midnight) or the *graveyard* shift (midnight to 8:00 a.m.) to regulate daytime hours. The daytime hours are slower and are usually the province of the older officers. The younger officer is usually unhappy when he is assigned to work *on days.* As an aside, it might be speculated that some of this action orientation could at times dictate the direction which emotionally charged situations take, as action often begets reaction.

In any event a police officer finds it rather incongruous that an agency purported to help people in trouble is closed after 5:00 p.m. and on weekends. Who gets into trouble during normal working hours on weekdays? And how come so few agencies have anything resembling home visits? The officer sees many people who will never go to an agency—perhaps this is a reason some agencies don't stay open.

Police are very responsible people. They hear, vaguely, that psychiatrists, social workers and psychologists are somehow concerned about emotionally disturbed people. Yet the police seldom see these professionals making an effort to get involved with the kinds of problems they are forced to face. They view this as irresponsibility, on the part of the professionals. There is a credibility gap, and this partly accounts for the fact that police seldom make referrals to or communicate with established agencies.

We hope it is no shock to learn that police have no great love or respect for us mental health professionals. Our unofficial rank order of professional groups disliked by police is as follows: (1) lawyers and judges; (2) doctors, especially psychiatrists; (3) social workers (usually equated with welfare workers); and (4) teachers. These groups are often seen as critical of the police without an attempt at understanding or support. These groups have many *bleeding hearts* who make good livings in relatively nice surroundings, leaving all the dirty work to the police. Living in their own safe offices, courtrooms and classrooms, where are these *know-it-alls* at 2:00 a.m.? Sunday mornings when the battle is raging?

Are the police wrong in their judgment of us? We would hope they are at least partly so. Certainly their understanding of us needs to be improved. We have found them as a group to be quite clannish and suspicious of *outsiders* who are not police. There is a constant refrain that no one can understand the police but police. The closed system and antagonism have become almost intolerable for us at times, especially when we are dealing with older officers.

But it would be unwise to pass off the accusation of hypocrisy in other groups as a problem of police closeness. There is some justification of their complaints that mental health professionals often pontificate on the basis of an incomplete picture. Two examples will illustrate this:

(1) We have tried to include mental health professionals as participants in our monthly forty hour seminars for police entitled *Understanding People*. One activity of these seminars is the role playing of scripts written by the participants. One such scene was that of a family fight that the officers were called to mediate:

Based on our patrol car experience, it was not a rare scene. The scene involved the loud shouting of obscenities, some violent shoving and some blood-curdling yells. It was very frightening but not unrealistic.

A very competent and experienced social worker who was a participating member of the group jumped up and shouted, "Is this for real?" Shaking somewhat he explained that he was very upset by the scene, and that in many years of working with disturbed families in his office he had never witnessed anything so unnerving. He didn't want them to continue the role playing. The police chuckled at what they considered to be his naivete. They pride themselves as being quite knowledgeable about the most seamy side of life.

(2) One of us (C.F.) was in a patrol car called to control a *violent man.* Upon arriving the *counselling team* was confronted by a completely *beserk* individual ranting and raving in the darkness outside his home. Getting out of the car, the police officer greeted him gently. Screaming obscenities the man suddenly jumped the officer. In the resulting melee it took a number of officers and a nightstick to finally control the completely irrational man. The most tense moment came when the man grabbed an officer's gun in an attempt to shoot him.

The professional present prudently retreated and stood by thinking about a lecture he had once given the police on *alternatives to violence.* He also thought about what a great story of police brutality a casual passerby might conjure.

A follow-up investigation of this man indicated that he might be classified as an explosive personality, with some police contacts in the past under similar circumstances. He was usually normal enough, but occasionally when frustration built up, he would *just lose my head and blow.*

That night he was finally handcuffed and immediately settled down. By the time he reached the jail he was very penitent and claimed amnesia for much of what had happened. He was not taken to a psychiatric facility because that route had been unsuccessfully tried in the past. The subdued subject had been turned away as *not psychotic or a danger now.*

In the instance reported a judge dismissed the case with a

minor penalty. The judge was not convinced that this situation was serious enough to force treatment. The subject explained it all on *a bad temper*—"I'll try to control it in the future." The man is on the street again, and the police are waiting for the next outbreak. They feel deserted.

Neither the judge or the admitting doctor in the past appreciated the potential danger in the situation. But how can such things be communicated? The professional present had dealt with such cases before, in his office, but never had he really felt what he did when he was part of the scene in the *raw*.

Perhaps it could be argued that the police mystique of violence was partly responsible for the explosiveness shown by the subjects described in both cases. A lot more study would have to be done, however, before this speculation could be made with any certainty.

Left to their own devices, police have developed many of their own techniques to deal with specific kinds of interpersonal problems. Some of these would be anathema to the absent professional, but they do work to alleviate the immediate problem. Some examples of this police inventiveness will be given, to illustrate the situations they find themselves.

Hallucinating people commonly call the police to *get those voices out of my attic* or to *take those little men out of my living room*. Police are not aware of the refinements of differential diagnosis and are not concerned about the effects of entering a subject's unreal world. Often they react in a very concrete manner. They do just what the person wants. They pretend to enter the hallucinating (or delusional) person's world and agree with the unreality. Once an officer went to great lengths of *capturing* some *little men*, ceremoniously put them into a bag and took them away. The elderly lady was apparently satisfied, as she did not call back.

Family fights are a real dread of the police officer. There is usually alcohol involved, and the situation can be dangerous for the officer. If an attempt to either get the warring parties to calm down or to separate for the night is unsuccessful, it is not unheard of for the officer to somehow seduce one member of the pair (usually the man) into hitting the other. Then an arrest can be made, and that's that!

Until recently public drunkenness was a crime. Thus, there has been a simple solution to any kind of disturbance in which an inebriated party is involved. Just get the person to *step outside,* to become *public,* and *away he goes to jail.* A new alcohol detoxification center here now offers an alternative.

One of the most intriguing stories of police inventiveness involved an officer who was being pestered with calls from an unmarried young relative who was convinced that people were following her home and looking into her window. After becoming convinced that the fears were groundless, the officer questioned the woman at length. He intuitively became suspicious about diet pills she was taking. He urged her to stop taking the pills for awhile, but she refused. He finally was able to examine the pills. The label on the bottle had been removed and she would not tell him the name of the prescribing doctor. He did note that they were very similar in size, shape and color to aspirin. Returning home he then very painstakingly filed the *A* off a corresponding number of aspirin tablets. On a subsequent visit to his relative, he surreptitiously substituted the modified aspirin tablets for the diet pills. Her paranoid reaction to amphetamines promptly disappeared.

We do not wish to imply that these techniques are standard operating procedures and are used regularly. They are used at times, however, for want of any better tools. It would be easy to be appalled at these methods. Where have we been, though, while they were being developed?

The main theme of this section has been that we think mental health professionals have by and large deserted police officers, who are significant mental health care givers for a portion of the population which is unserved by the usual agencies.

We have alluded to police clannishness, and it might be argued that the real problem lies in the unwillingness of the police to ask for help. Certainly we have as often felt unwelcome as welcome in our work with police, and a strong argument could be made for this.

In looking at basics, however, we have to think that the primary responsibility for establishing contact with the police lies with those specified as mental health professionals. We are the ones who have designated ourselves as custodians of the nation's mental health. The work may be very unpleasant but we cannot turn our collective backs on the police and those who in an obtuse way are calling for help.

Police Culture and the Helping Process

Fortier (1972), a policeman, has written about the typical behavior of the police as a group, which he terms *police culture.* Fortier stresses such characteristics as cynicism about people, isolation from nonpolice, an exaggerated group coalescence, an intense fascination with and dedication to the job, and defensiveness about criticism.

In this section we will comment on some of our observations of the police culture as directly related to the aiding of people in interpersonal crisis.

Police see as a main demand of their job that they *be in control* of any situation they encounter. Ambiguity about who is in charge is difficult for them. Yet how does one control emotionally boiling human interactions such as a family disturbance or a psychotic break? For the officer this often means using the solution that is most readily available—a common one is arrest. He knows how to operate within the arrest procedure, and in this sense he can control.

Combined with this are the personal dangers of an involvement with another human being. During a shift many different demands, of a variable quality, are made on an officer. With much pressure already, an attempt at communication on an emotional level can be, to use a cliche—the straw that breaks the camel's back. We have noted that many officers who can stoically face physical assault or the threat of such, will comment with some envy about our ability to take emotional risks.

We believe that real control of human problem situations comes only from an ability and willingness to take both physical and emotional risks. While we are often at a loss in helping police with specific techniques to deal with specific situations, we think we have been helpful in introducing them to the world of emotions.

Contributing, also, to both the policeman's human relations contacts and his isolation from the community is the concept of

Out of Service Time (OST). This is the term that is used to sig-
nify when an officer is absent from his patrol car. He is *In Service*
when he is actively patrolling. This stems from a common belief
that *real* police work deals with matters of crime, such as appre-
hending the burglar or the armed robber. The *human* side of
police work only takes time away from these real concerns.

We have heard, often, that police officers do not have the
time to do *social work*. It has been our experience, however,
that boredom, resulting from the significant free time the patrolling officer has, is a big problem in maintaining morale. Still
the belief persists that the officer must not obligate himself for
more than a brief period to any kind of human problem, since he
must be back *In Service* should a *hot call* arise.

In approaching human problem situations, police often view
themselves as *con artists* trying to bring about a quick resolution.
This term has a better connotation to them than the more socially disapproved term of social worker. It seems to us that the
sensitivity required to produce good results as a con artist is not
too dissimilar from what is required to be a good social worker.
We have continually been impressed with the *street-wise* knowledge of some officers. One older officer, for example, described
his basic rule gleaned from many years of experience in terms
of *never taking away a man's self-respect*. He could describe
numerous situations in which he had helped others and simplified
the job for himself by operating on this basic philosophy. Yet
in speaking of himself as a con artist, it seems to us that the
policeman is downgrading the importance of conscious understanding.

The police mystique is a very masculine one, whereas, feelings
are often equated with femininity. Thus there are feelings about
feelings which have to be dealt with in any attempt to increase
awareness.

It should be realistically noted that the human side of law enforcement work can also be physically dangerous. A large per-
centage of the physical injuries and deaths of police officers
occur in the category of family disturbances. Officers will explain
that in this and in other human problem calls they are at least
able to prepare and predict what is going to occur. On a *robbery*

in progress the officer has a much better awareness of the possibilities and therefore feels better prepared to plan and later cope with them.

To deal with uncertainty, officers often make a strong attempt to stereotype human problems, so as to have a simple solution. This is what is often sought from us—a simple solution to a very complex problem. Once we are able to work through the anger directed at us for not having simple solutions, there is often envy at our ability to live with ambiguity and even confusion.

Another aspect of the police culture which has a bearing on their involvement in human problems is what might be called, immediacy. By this we mean, problems are considered only in their current context and in a very time-limited focus. This has already been touched upon in a mention of arrest as a common quick solution. Such thinking can, of course, work to police disadvantage in the long run. One such recent example of this occurred when an individual in a drunk, angry, disturbed state had to be disarmed. The manner in which this was accomplished left him quite resentful. A week and a half later, some other officers had to repeat the task, and they had a much more dangerous adversary to contend with, on this second contact.

We have seen evidence of the so-called *police image.* Often, however, we are distressed to find that this concern is more with how one looks in a given situation rather than how the problem situation itself might be improved. Again there is the emphasis on immediacy rather than any long range prevention.

This concept of prevention cannot be minimized, especially in regard to children. We have been involved in many situations where children watch helplessly while their parents violently reenact some chronic family problem, with the only help available being the police who were called by neighbors who couldn't stand the noise. These impressionable children can form ideas of the police as helpers or just extensions of the problem. This has many implications regarding their own behavior toward police, in years to come. Although their actions sometimes belie this, police are concerned about this problem. We have heard them say that they live or die in each others *heat.*

We have been impressed that many people involved with the

police as helpers, despite much current publicity about the bad police image. We have also been impressed that the help wanted is clearly, nonverbal in form. We saw a number of individuals, for example, who clearly were using violent arrest as a means of reestablishing a masculine self-image. Another, a woman, frustrated by one of our officer pupil's experimenting with an empathetic approach, succinctly advised him, "Don't give me any of that psychological crap."

The police are called with the expectation that they will solve often *unsolvable problems.* This is certainly something they have in common with the mental health professional. Rather than confront the people involved with the complexity of the problem, police tend to follow their own action-orientation and take some action. They *give in* to the expectations of those who called for help.

In the absence of much help from professionals, the police have been doing *Okay.* Primarily, they have been performing a holding action. If the mental health of our society is to improve, more carefully devised methods of dealing with common police problems will have to be forthcoming. These methods will have to emphasize long term effects, will have to involve police, and mental health professionals working together.

In this section we have given some of our observations of the police culture and its effects on the helping process. We hope they will be useful to other professionals who are or will be working with police.

Summary and Conclusions

Our main theme in this chapter has been that the police officer is a significant mental health care giver, especially for that more nonverbal, action-oriented element of our society to those who seem unable to utilize more traditional helping agencies—or if they have, it has not been helpful. We have further contended that mental health professionals have too long allowed the police officer to struggle with these problems by himself. The responsibility for initiating communication rests primarily with the professional.

We have described our program of police training, consultation and service in some detail. We have also stressed our problems in entering the police system which we view as quite closed. When all is said and done, we think that our main contributions will be in opening the system, and in starting a dialogue between police and mental health professionals. The specific techniques used to achieve those ends are relatively unimportant.

We do think that anyone working with police will first have to become a student, learn from them. Patrol car riding is almost a *sine qua non* in this regard. The person will also have to develop a thick hide and learn to withstand a lot of collective antagonism. There is a continual demand to prove oneself.

In training situations we have found small group discussions and action techniques (e.g., role playing, interviewing actual patients, etc.) far superior to formal lectures. We have also found that breaking up the training day with field trips is very helpful. Getting in a car and going someplace seems to recreate for the officer an on-the-job situation, and brings about a certain anxiety and involvement. We have used actors in various simulated scenes, but have been most gratified with the use of police themselves as script writers and actors. As has been pointed out to us, police have to put on different faces throughout their working day, and therefore are good actors.

We have found certain characteristics of the police culture to be particular problems in their trying to help people with human problems. These include the need for control, the concept of *Out of Service Time*, the suspicion of feelings, and the desire for immediate results. It is in initiating and encouraging examination of these issues in a permissive atmosphere that we think the mental health professional can offer most to the police system. This implies, of course, that the professional will teach most by example, in humbly venturing forth from his own safe surroundings into a different world.

We think the professional also has something to offer in terms of providing direct service in conjunction with the police. Emphross and French (1972) have written of three ways in which this might be done. They speak of training police as paraprofessionals, of having a crisis team of mental health workers within a department, and of more encouragement for police to call upon social agencies to pick up on appropriate situations.

We are experimenting with a fourth way that we think is unparallelled in its opportunity for cooperation and cross fertilization. We, as professionals, pair with a police officer to form a counselling team. The main work is being done by our three graduate social work students from Portland State University. With their regular officer partner, each of these students provides after-hours coverage during one night a week for the Multnomah County Sheriffs Department. The main problem is that frequently, the students have not been busy enough. Barriers of all kinds are breaking down, however, and everyone involved is enthusiastic. Secondary gains occur since the students are carrying back to the school a clear picture of just what the officer is up against, while the officers are learning that the *pros* can tolerate much confusion and uncertainty.

In conclusion we hope that more professionals from other disciplines, especially mental health people, will involve themselves with the police and their problems. First, all of us have to become students.

REFERENCES

1. Bard, A.: Training Police as Specialists in Family Crisis Intervention. Final Report of Project OLEA #157. Washington, D.C., U.S. Department of Justice, 1970.
2. Ephross, P., and French, Patricia.: Social Service and the Police. *Hospital and Community Psychiatry, 23*: 61-63, 1972.
3. Fortier, K.: The Police Culture—It's Effect on Sound Police—Community Relations. *Police Chief 39*: 33-35, 1972.
4. Mazer, M.: Two Ways of Expressing Psychological Disorder: The Experience of a Demarcated Population. *Amer J. Psychiatry 128*: 933-938, 1972.
5. The Portland Police Officer. Report of Portland State University Urban Studies Center. Portland, Oregon, Portland State College, 1967.
6. Wilson, J.: *Varieties of Police Behavior.* Cambridge, Harvard University Press, 1968.

SECTION FIVE
A LOOK TO THE FUTURE

CHAPTER XIII

NEW DOORS, NOT
OLD WALLS

JOHN N. MITCHELL[1]

L ET ME JOIN THE OTHERS in welcoming you to this National
Conference on Corrections. As many of you know, this conference stems from the continuing concern over prison reform
by the President of the United States, and is a part of the national
corrections program that he set in motion two years ago.

In 1969 President Nixon directed his Administration to pursue
correctional reform along thirteen specific avenues. He also
appointed a Task Force on Prisoner Rehabilitation, which made
a number of significant recommendations in April, 1970.

Together, these directives and recommendations represent the
most determined and comprehensive approach to corrections ever
made in this country. I refer not only to Federal corrections, but
insofar as the Federal Government can provide, funds, training
and leadership, this approach is a Magna Carta of prison reform
for all levels of government.

We are here to review how far we have come in implementing
the reforms already proposed by the President and others, and
to chart a course over the vast sea of problems remaining.

Until the last two years, it could be said of prison reform what
Mark Twain is supposed to have said about the weather: "Everybody talks about it, but nobody ever does anything about it."

---

[1] This chapter is based on a talk given by the Attorney General at the National
Conference on Corrections, Williamsburg, Virginia, Dec. 6, 1971.

Some of the talking was done at a National Congress on Penitentiary and Reformatory Discipline, meeting in Cincinnati. Among other things, it recommended that:

> The prime goal of prisons is not to punish, but to reform.
> Prison personnel should be much better trained and developed to professional status.
> Prisoners should be classified and treated appropriately and separately.
> They should be handled with incentives and moral suasion, not physical punishment.
> They should be given hope of reduced sentence and parole for good behavior.
> Their academic education and vocational training should receive primary emphasis.
> They should be helped to find their way in society after release.

When were these enlightened ideas proposed? Not last month or last year, but 1870—more than a century ago.

Forty years ago a National Commission on Law Observance and Enforcement, known as the Wickersham Commission, devoted an entire volume of its report to the subject of corrections. Among its recommendations were the very same ones that had already been recommeneded in 1870.

Nearly five years ago a President's Commission on Law Enforcement and Administration of Justice devoted a chapter of its final report to corrections. Among its recommendations were ones previously made in 1870 and 1931.

What was the result of this century of recommendations?

In state after state, most of the prisons have no programs for correcting the prisoner. Only a fraction of inmates in the country are exposed to such programs.

Only from 10 to 20 percent of all prison system budgets in this country is spent on actual programs to correct the inmate; the rest is spent on custody and administration.

Only 20 percent of institutional personnel are assigned to correctional type programs.

In many states, first offenders are mingled with hardened criminals; in many cases, juveniles are mingled with adults.

In any other profession this kind of neglect would be unthinkable. How would we react if a hospital put accident victims in the Communicable Disease Ward—and at that, a ward in which the patient received a bed, but no treatment? We should be just as appalled at the situation in many of our prisons today. Little wonder that, in sounding the call for prison reform, President Nixon declared, "The American system for correcting and rehabilitating criminals presents a convincing case of failure."

There are of course, some outstanding exceptions. But in characterizing most American prisons I need only use the same language that the Wickersham Commission used forty years ago:

> We conclude that the present prison system is antiquated and inefficient. It does not reform the criminal. It fails to protect society. There is reason to believe that it contributes to the increase of crime by hardening the prisoner.

Today we have figures to confirm that belief. According to the FBI, those arrested on Federal Criminal charges in 1970 had an average of four prior criminal arrests and an average of nearly 1½ convictions at the local, state or federal level. The nearly 38,-000 persons arrested on federal charges in 1970 had a total of more than 22,000 prior imprisonments of six months or longer in one type of institution or another.

These and many other studies with similar results should not surprise me. It is as simple as the words of the novelist, Dostoyevsky: ". . . neither convict prisons, nor prison ships, nor any system of hard labor ever cured a criminal."

The fact is that other trends in American life are going to make this corrections problem even more pressing in the future. The trend toward improved law enforcement systems will not only deter crime in the long run, but in the near term one of its effects should be to increase the arrest rate. Moreover, if the court reform movement proceeds as we hope, it will speed the prosecution of more defendants. Together, these two factors will send many more offenders through the criminal justice system, thus putting added strain on the corrections program.

We must be prepared for this new wave of offenders coming into the prison system—ready not just with added beds and benches, but ready to make the most of an opportunity to reach a large number of offenders with modern correction techniques.

At the same time, the rising level of education in the United States is leaving a bigger gap between the undereducated offender and society at large. So our job training and educational programs in the prisons must be pushed even harder to keep up with successes in other aspects of society.

Recognizing that there are many successful corrections programs by various jurisdictions, I would like to examine briefly the particular program developed in response to President Nixon's directions two years ago.

First, the President's program has received growing financial support from Congress, thanks to some dedicated leaders in the corrections crusade such as Senator Roman L. Hruska of Nebraska. Funds specifically earmarked for corrections, over and above the other corrections grants, have been added to the program of Law Enforcement Assistant Administration, part of the Department of Justice.

Second, in 1970 the Interagency Council on Corrections was created to focus the work of all relevant Federal agencies on prisoner rehabilitation. This consists of representatives from a dozen agencies within the Departments of Justice, Labor, Defense, and Health, Education and Welfare, as well as from the Department of Housing and Urban Development, the Office of Economic Opportunity, and the U.S. Civil Service Commission.

Third, the United States Board of Parole was reorganized in 1969 to enable Parole Hearing Examiners to conduct many of the hearings in correctional institutions across the country. This permits the Board members to devote more time to the decision making process and to hold more appellate reviews.

Fourth, the Federal Bureau of Prisons within the Department of Justice developed a comprehensive ten year master plan to improve the effectiveness of the Federal Prison System and hopefully to make it a model of correctional endeavor for other agencies in this country to follow. This plan emphasizes individualized treatment and community orientation. The Bureau has already made a good start in achieving these goals, particularly in two vital areas—personnel training and new facilities.

The first regional staff training center was opened last January. It provides professional training to develop the correctional officer as an agent for change rather than as primarily a custodian or keeper. The second regional training center will be opened the first of this coming year, and three more are planned for the future. As soon as possible, these facilities will also be made available to state and local correctional personnel.

This month the Bureau plans to break ground for its first Metropolitan Correctional Center in New York City. This multi-purpose facility will provide presentence and postsentence short-term detention, diagnostic service to the courts, prerelease services to the offenders returning to the city from other institutions, and correctional services for parolees and probationers. Construction will begin on a similar center in Chicago in June, 1972, and six other centers are scheduled for urban areas where the need is most acute.

Construction will begin early next year on a facility unique in correctional practice. This is the Behavioral Research Center at Butner, North Carolina, which will provide treatment for and research on special groups of offenders, including the mentally disturbed. And in the fiscal 1972 budget, Congress provided for construction of a West Coast complex of facilities in four metropolitan areas to provide better correctional techniques for youthful offenders.

Fifth, the Law Enforcement Assistance Administration has greatly increased its funding for correctional aid to the states and localities. In fiscal 1971 this reached $178,000,000, which included more than $47 million in Part E funds that Congress for the first time, especially earmarked for corrections, at the urging of President Nixon. This Part E funding has been more than doubled in the current 1972 fiscal year, bringing the total LEAA funding for corrections in this current year to nearly a quarter of billion dollars. For the first time, substantial funds are available for a coordinated program to bring American penology into the twentieth Century.

From its inception, the entire LEAA corrections program has had a common theme—preparing the offender for assimilation into society. One reason is that community-based programs are within the financial reach of the Federal assistance program and of the states and localities. If these correctional programs are as successful as we hope, we may not need to build all the new facilities that now seem to be required by the antiquated condition of most penal institutions. Some funds are being used for construction, but on a very selective basis which emphasizes corrections, not just detention. Already, as a result of LEAA funding, we can see some visible areas of progress. To cite only a few:

> Kentucky has begun its first organized prerelease program for prison inmates.
> Arizona has begun treatment programs in county jails.
> Michigan is developing a million-dollar model program to treat young offenders in community-based programs.
> Missouri is opening twelve new community treatment centers for offenders and ex-offenders and thirty-six homes for juveniles.
> Louisiana is building a state institution for women and two regional centers for offenders.
> Indiana has opened two new regional centers for juveniles in the past two years and will open four more.
> Florida is implementing a major probation program for juveniles directed by the state.
> New York is launching a massive series of professional training programs for existing correctional personnel at all levels.

Those programs are only a fraction of the whole picture.

Last Fiscal year LEAA put over $2 million into job training and placement programs operated by private industry.

LEAA has also made direct grants to cities and counties to finance community treatment centers, narcotics and drug treatment, job placement, juvenile probation, work release, group homes, rehabilitation of alcoholics, halfway houses, volunteer aid programs, psychiatric care, and a host of other offender rehabilitation efforts.

We are also aware that many states need technical advice on how their facilities need improving, and even on how their new buildings should be designed to make maximum use of modern correctional methods. I am able to announce that, to meet this need, LEAA has funded a National Clearinghouse for Criminal Justice Architecture at the University of Illinois.

Professional assistance in planning and implementing education programs for inmates is also a need of many states and localities. For this purpose I am today directing LEAA to establish a National Clearing house for Correctional Education, using such funds as are now available for its initial phase of development. This Clearinghouse will give technical help, including curriculum planning and classroom and correspondence course materials, to correctional agencies establishing education programs for primary through college level.

These are only a few highlights, and they do not include numerous research programs to advance the science of corrections.

Already, because this large LEAA funding is now available, state and local correctional administrators have begun to press for change. They are documenting their needs, with new confidence that those needs will be met. No longer are they voices in the wilderness.

In addition, other Federal agencies are providing strong support. At three Federal institutions, the Office of Economic Opportunity has funded programs to prepare selected inmates for advanced educational opportunities. A number of vocational training courses for handicapped inmates have been sponsored by the Rehabilitation Services Administration of HEW. The Manpower Administration of the Department of Labor has made numerous grants to provide occupational training for inmates of Federal, state and local institutions. And the Manpower Administration is also participating with United States Attorneys and the Federal Courts in a program to provide jobs and correctional guidance to selected defendants, without trial.

Recently, steps have been taken to bring even closer coordination of Federal and state corrections programs.

A National Advisory Commission on Criminal Justice Standards and Goals, chaired by Governor Russell Peterson of Delaware, has been established by LEAA. Among the standards it will consider and establish are those for corrections. I trust that when these are forthcoming, correctional institutions at all levels will give them the most serious consideration, to the end that all such American institutions can work toward the same goals.

In addition, the cabinet heads of the Department of Justice Labor, and HEW last week joined in sending a letter to the governors of all states and territories, offering fresh technical and financial assistance in a coordinated federal-state program for correction of offenders. Grants for preparation of plans will be made to all participating states before the end of this fiscal year. Some time in February the representatives designated by the Governors will meet with Federal officials in Washington to agree upon guidelines for the program plans. The result will be that the states can make comprehensive plans with the assurance that they will receive substantial Federal financial support starting in fiscal 1973.

So we have here the first major step in articulating and implementing a national program—federal, state and local—on the correction of offenders. I hope that your deliberations here will provide a body of professional recommendations that will guide state and Federal planners.

In short, a number of factors have combined to give us the best opportunity in this century to bring some genuine reform to the most neglected aspect of our society.

> We have concerned and enlightened leadership—a President who has made prison reform one of the priorities of his Administration.
> We have significant funds available and aviable program for allocating them.
> We have some outstanding examples of progress in both state and Federal prison institutions.
> We have a higher level of public support than ever before.

For the first time, we can mount a national corrections program that does not simply repair old buildings, and is not based only on old concepts of restraint and deterrence. Instead we can make use of the imaginative corrections principles that have been advocted for at least a century.

More than this, we can be bold enough to consider new ideas. Let me close by sharing just a few with you.

First, as you know, the need for better training and common performance standards among correctional officials is shared by all government levels. In this connection I am today directing the Federal Bureau of Prisons and the LEAA to work with the states and localities in establishing a National Corrections Academy. This would serve as a national center for correctional learning, research, executive seminars, and development of correctional policy recommendations. It would cover the whole range of correctional disciplines, from the new employee to the manageement level. Besides giving professional training of the highest quality, it would provide a continuing meeting ground for the exchange of advanced ideas on corrections. I believe it will be the most effective single means of upgrading the profession and assuring that correction is more than a euphemism for detention. I hope that the members of this Conference will give us the benefit of their ideas on implementing this Academy in the most effective way.

Second, I call upon all agencies to increase minority employment among professional correctional personnel. In my opinion this would greatly increase the effectiveness of counseling and guidance at all stages of the corrections process. Practically all prison systems, including the Federal system, have a long way to go in this regard. I am pleased to report that the Director of the Federal Bureau of Prisons has directed all twenty-eight federal institutions to work toward a goal of one-third minority employment in all new hiring. I urge corrections institutions at all levels to make an extraordinary effort to find and recruit minority personnel—not only because it is the law, not only because it is fair, but because it can genuinely benefit the corrections process. LEAA is already funding a program to aid police departments in increasing their proportion of minority officers, and I am today directing LEAA to expand this program to include the same aid for correctional systems.

Third, let us recognize that correction should begin, not with the prisons, but with the courts. Let us ask whether in every case we need to achieve *the object so sublime* of the Mikado's Lord High Executioner— "To make the punishment fit the crime." In many cases, society can best be served by diverting the accused to a voluntary community-oriented correctional program instead of bringing him to trial. The federal criminal justice system has already used this formula in many juvenile cases—the so-called Brooklyn plan. I believe this program could be expanded to include certain offenders beyond the juvenile age, without losing the general deterrent effect of the criminal justice system. I am therefore directing the Executive Office of United States Attorneys and the Criminal Division of the Justice Department to study the feasibility of enlarging the area of criminal cases in which the prosecutor might be justified in deferring prosecution in favor of an immediate community-oriented correction program.

Finally, I propose for your consideration a more general problem—the need to elevate public attitudes toward the release. Studies have shown an appalling resistance to hiring ex-offenders, even by many governmental agencies at different levels, thus frustrating other efforts at correction. Some state laws prohibit the hiring of ex-offenders by government agencies, however well-adjusted or corrected they may be. When such a release is thus denied the means of making an honest living, every sentence becomes a life sentence. The attitude of each citizen toward salvaging offenders as valuable human beings is one of the obvious cases covered by the popular saying, "If you're not part of the solution, you're part of the problem."

It is my hope that as the rehabilitation approach to penology begins to work, the public will begin to change its archaic feeling about exoffenders. The public's predominant impression of penology will be, not of old walls, but of new doors. And this in turn can be the final breakthrough in the centuries-old battle to reclaim and assimilate the ex-offender.

Winston Churchill once said that attitudes toward the treatment of criminals are "one of the unfailing tests of the civilization of any country." Let us do all in our power to assure that our country may yet be able to meet this test, not in shame, but with pride.

Ladies and gentlemen, I wish to thank you for your participation in this Conference. We are counting on your counsel as we enter a new phase in a national correctional program, and I trust that your dedication to this cause will produce some truly inspired guidance that is equal to the challenge.

SUBJECT INDEX

Academic preparation, correctional counselor, 64-66

Adjustment area, tip to newspaper editor, 63

Administration, correctional programs, 10-18

Administrators,
abilities needed, 11-12
responsibilities and procedures, 15-16

Adolescents,
special attention needed, 15-16
virtue characteristics, 86

Adult prisoners, childhood law breakers, 6-7

Adults, virtue characteristics, 86

African Culture Group, counselor's rapport with, 67-68

Agency personnel, responsibilities, 13

Alcoholics,
inmates, psychologist's programs for, 66
men on work release, 132
rehabilitation,
LEAA funding aid, 204
possibility, 25

Alcoholics Anonymous, aid to inmate, 121

Alternatives to prison, 6
work release program, 27

America,
crime's significance, 85-86
women prisoner aid, 75-76

American Corrections Associations, informational material, 16

American prison system, failure, 5

Amphetamines, paranoid reactions, 189

Antabuse, alcohol problem use, 136-137

Antisocial conduct,
predictability, 7

prevention, public's role, 15
psychiatric prediction, 7
set patterns, 13

Arizona treatment program, 204

Arkansas Penetentiary System, condemned by court, 33

Armed robbery, society threatened, 24

Arrest, description by suspect, 112-113

Assaults on inmates, protection lacking in Arkansas Penetentiary, 33

Attica prison riot, 64

Auburn system, descipline and labor, 31

Authoritarian quality, correctional institutions, 61

Authority, improving attitude toward, 133

Backstabbing, guard class behavior, 61

Bail Reform Act, effects, 36-37

Behavior changes,
correction administrator's aid, 13
environmental reinforcement essential, 69

Behavior control problems, temporary incarceration, 71

Behavioral Research Center, North Carolina, 203

Behavioral science, correctional counselor, study, 64

Berrigan, Daniel and Phillip, influence on prisoners, 59

Bias, women's incarceration, 78

Bible reading, inmate's account, 171-172

Black Muslim movement, relation to prisoner attitude change, 59

Black Panthers, relation to prisoner attitude change, 59

Born to lose syndrome, avoidance, 13

NAME INDEX